THE COMPLETE
CRUISE
Handbook

YOUR PORTHOLE COMPANION TO THE WORLD OF CRUISES

BY ANNE VIPOND

**OCEAN
CRUISE
GUIDES**

Vancouver, Canada • San Clemente, USA

Published by:
Ocean Cruise Guides Ltd.
614 - 888 Beach Avenue
Vancouver, BC V6Z 2P9
(604) 685-0593   Fax (604) 685-2479

Publisher/Managing Editor: William Kelly
Copy Editor: Mel-Lynda Andersen
Cover Artwork: Alan Nakano
Cover Design: Hoy Jacobsen & Co.
Production: Foley FX Graphix Inc., Vancouver
Printed by Hignell Printers, Winnipeg, Manitoba

Canadian Cataloguing in Publication Data

Vipond Anne, 1957 -
 The complete cruise handbook

Includes index.
ISBN 0-9697991-1-X

1.Ocean travel – Guidebooks. 2. Cruise Ships - Guidebooks. I Title.
G550. V56 1996   910.4'5   C95-911246-4

Printed in Canada

A t one time, the idea of vacationing at sea conjured images of white tie and tails, and glittery gowns. Fred Astaire and Ginger Rogers danced among the rich and glamorous while the elderly, snugly tucked in lap robes, sipped bouillon on sheltered decks. Cruising was a vacation for the indolent rich, not to be contemplated by anyone whose luggage did not match or whose wardrobe was made by the wrong designer. Nor was cruising a choice for the active traveler – not if exercise more vigorous than shuffleboard was sought.

During those early years, cruise vacations built a solid reputation based on caring and attentive service, opulent surroundings, fine dining and world-spanning adventure. A cruise was an elegant experience, offering comfort and convenience unparalleled by any other vacation option.

As the industry evolved to its modern form, cruise lines – sensitive to the changing tastes and lifestyles of today's vacationers – distilled the essence of the glamorous past and added to the mix the flavors and textures of contemporary leisure activities.

In a setting that reflects today's more casual and healthy lifestyle, cruise vacationers feast from menus that both tempt the palate and care for their nutritional well being. Activities aboard the industry's fleet also reflect an understanding of society's less sedentary pursuits. Health clubs and spas now rival the best ashore. Life enrichment programs, guest lecturers, culinary training and other skill developments, in a range of interests, all insure that the mind as well as the body is nurtured as part of the rich cruise vacation experience.

Today's cruise vacation, like never before, offers a wide variety of choices. Itineraries span the globe: from the tropical splendor of the Caribbean to the scenic grandeur of Alaska. Picturesque Bermuda, the Hawaiian Islands, and the capitals of Europe, are only a small sample of the choices that make up the extensive menu of vacations by sea. Quick three-night getaways, seven-night vacations, classic epic voyages, and everything in between, make up today's cruising universe. From the eminently affordable to the most luxurious, there is a cruise vacation that will enthrall every vacationer and make each of them feel like they've joined the ranks of the glamorous privileged few who walked the decks of cruise ships of the past.

I hope that after reading this book you are encouraged, enthused and ready to experience all that a cruising vacation has to offer.

Albert C. Wallack
Chairman
Cruise Lines International Association

ACKNOWLEDGMENTS

The following organizations kindly supplied photography for this book and their assistance is acknowledged with gratitude.

Alaska Sightseeing/Cruise West 38, 57 (bottom), 77 (middle), 125; Carnival Cruise Lines 107, 162 (Andy Newman),167; Celebrity Cruises 17, 108, 109; Crystal Cruises 110, 134; Cunard Cruises 39, 110, 112; Delta Queen Steamboat Company 90, 129; Fenwick & Lang 94; Holland America Line 113, 114, 142; Hong Kong Tourist Authority 77; Norwegian Cruise Line 58 (bottom), 59 (bottom), 89, 116, 117; P&O Cruises 133, 141; Princess Cruises 20 (top), 33, 64, 77 (bottom), 79 (middle), 119, 168; Royal Caribbean Cruise Line 25, 39, 98 (bottom), 121, 122, 165, 166; Seabourn Cruise Line 123, 170; Thomas Cook Group Ltd. 37 (bottom); Tourism Vancouver 78; Windstar Cruises 38, 125 (Gary Nolton).

We also thank the following individuals for supplying us with photographs: Fred Jensen 17 (bottom), 118; Raymond Norris-Jones 54; Gordon Persson 7, 40 (bottom), 43, 47, 57 (top), 63, 103 (bottom); Nan Short 19 (middle).

All other photography is by Anne Vipond.

One of the best ways to see the world is by cruise ship. Not only is cruising a carefree mode of travel that leaves you relaxed and refreshed to enjoy each port of call, no other type of vacation receives a higher rate of customer satisfaction. The majority of first-time cruisers report that their inaugural cruise didn't simply fulfill their expectations, it exceeded them. The reason for this is the diversity of cruising. Passengers who like to be active can partake in a packed schedule of daily events both at sea and in port, while those who prefer quieter pastimes can simply recline in a deck chair and gaze at the passing scenery.

More than five million North American vacationers took a cruise last year – many of them for the first time. However, despite the growing popularity of cruise vacations, the number of people choosing to cruise remains a small percentage of the total tourism market. Cruise vacations have yet to become a mainstream holiday, with many people perceiving cruises as being stuffy, expensive, sedate or boring. These misconceptions are based on what cruising was like in the past, not the present reality. In recent years the cruise industry has transformed itself, and what was once an exclusive type of holiday has become an affordable and all-inclusive vacation package. Today's modern ships come in a wide range of sizes and styles, and offer an impressive array of optional activities, both on board and on shore.

Nonetheless, it's only natural to be skeptical about the unfamiliar. Those who have never cruised may think that cruise travel has nothing to offer except lineups and regimented routines. Then they embark on a first cruise and their conversion is instant – but by no means unique. The adventure and allure of cruising begins the moment a person walks across the gangway and steps onto a ship. Greeted by smiling faces and smartly-attired stewards, each and every passenger feels special as they are welcomed aboard and shown to their cabins.

The excitement of embarkation is surpassed only by the euphoria that fills the air when the lines are released and the ship eases away from the dock. There's a remarkable sense of freedom as the bonds of land are broken and those left waving from shore wish they were the lucky ones at the ship's rail, experiencing that magical moment when a ship sets sail for distant lands.

Cruising delivers on both the adventure of travel and the relaxation of a pampered vacation. Passengers can visit the world's famous capitals and exotic ports of call, then retreat from the heat, hustle and bustle when they return to their ship – an oasis of calm and comfort wherever it may be docked.

This handbook has been designed to explain why cruising is one of the most satisfying modes of travel available to today's vacationer, and why cruise ships evoke a timeless appeal that is stronger than ever.

CHAPTER ONE

WHY CRUISE?

The Lure of a Shipboard Vacation

To cruise by ship to new destinations is to revisit youth. If you travel with an inquiring mind and a carefree heart, you will never be past the age of discovery. And there is so much of the world of cruising to discover: the morning sun on your face, the smell of fresh varnish on teak, the sound of chimes at dinner, and the sight of smartly-attired officers and crew running the ship. There is nothing for you to do but yield to the fortunate circumstances that brought you here, and enjoy. A cruise is a pause, a chance to reflect and look outward to the golden sky, the glistening sea, and all that surrounds you and your ship.

It is a well-advertised fact that cruising is one of the best value-for-money vacation packages available today. Your accommodation, meals, entertainment, and transportation to a number of destinations, are all included in the cost, which can be as low as $100 a day. But cruising's other benefits are more abstract. Since cruises were first introduced in England as a form of vacation travel in the 1840s, people have discovered there is something about the sea and salt air that is romantic, invigorating and, perhaps most important, relaxing. In the closing years of the 20th century there has never been such need for relief from the stress of modern life and finding a quiet sanctuary to recharge. A cruise, for many, provides this. With the highest level of customer satisfaction of any type of holiday, cruising has become the vacation of the 1990s and is poised for a period of strong, steady growth.

Individual passengers have their own reasons for cruising, and the following are some of the benefits most often cited by cruise enthusiasts.

The Ultimate in Pampering and Relaxation

We all need to occasionally 'get away from it all.' Cruising literally removes you from all land-based routines and places you in a novel setting that is stimulating yet familiar, soothing yet engaging.

Cruising is hassle free, crime free and stress free. Tired of making decisions? Envisage an evening at sea and its similarities to enjoying a night on the town at a popular holiday resort. Start with dinner at an elegant restaurant followed by a stage show, or dancing to a live band at a local club, or going to the cinema, or reclining in the corner seat of a piano bar, or browsing in the local shops, or trying your luck in the casino.

These are all activities you can enjoy on a cruise ship, but not once do you need to reach for your wallet, make a reservation, stand in a lineup, pay a cover charge at the door, hail a cab (or dodge a cab), hand someone a tip, park your car (once you've found a parking space) or drive back to your hotel in the dark along unfamiliar streets.

You can meander from venue to venue on board a ship. The operative word is flexibility – if none of the scheduled activities appeal to you any particular evening, you can simply go for a late-night stroll along the promenade deck, breathing in the fresh sea air before retiring to your cabin which your steward will have tidied while you were at dinner, replacing soiled towels with fresh ones, turning down your bed, perhaps even placing a good-night chocolate on your pillow.

Sound idyllic? There's more. Daytime on board a ship is equally relaxing and invigorating. There is nothing more exuberant than rising at dawn to stride the freshly scrubbed decks and feel the morning breeze on your face, then stroll to the lido deck for a casual breakfast by the pool or visit the main dining room for a full-course start to the day. Not a morning person? You can sleep until noon if you like – your steward won't disturb you. Or you can order breakfast in bed and watch the sun slowly gain control of the day. On a cruise, your time is your own.

This is one of the main advantages of taking a cruise – your day can be as whimsical or as planned as you like. The morning can be spent in a lounge chair by the swimming pool, dozing in the sunshine and going for a dip from time to time to cool off. Or you might prefer visiting the library, the beauty salon, or the gym for a vigorous workout to get some of that modern stress out of your system before sitting down to lunch. Whatever your definition of 'relaxation', it takes on its full meaning in the course of a cruise.

In our fast-paced world, cruising also provides the opportunity to slow down. No excuses are necessary to stretch out in a deck chair and indulge in daydreams as you gaze seaward at some billowy white clouds becalmed on a sea blue sky.

Attentive service and a relaxed atmosphere are hallmarks of modern-day cruising.

Family Freedom

As much as we value the company of loved ones, it's also essential to have some time to ourselves. On a cruise, couples and families can holiday together but still pursue their personal interests – both on board the ship and at each port of call.

For instance, one member of a couple may want to visit the casino after lunch while the other may decide to take in a film at the ship's cinema. Or you may be interested in attending a lecture while your partner prefers joining a table tennis tournament. It's easy to go your separate ways for a while, then rendezvous back at the cabin or in your favorite bar.

On board a ship, with its closed environment, there is the added benefit of security. Even at the ports of call, organized shore excursions by the cruise line ensure a high degree of safety so that one of you may choose to go on a city or island tour while the other can partake in a round of golf or an afternoon spent scuba diving. There are, of course, many things you will want to do together, as a couple or as a family, but the point remains that a cruise gives you many options.

Children and cruise ships go together very well. Adults cruising without children have reported that although the ship was carrying several hundred junior passengers, they hardly ever saw or heard them. The reason, a child might explain, is that when you're having this much fun who wants to hang around the adults? Many ships have excellent facilities for youngsters and teens, including sport competitions, scavenger hunts, and games with prizes. Some ships have special movies for children and teens, and parties with the kind of food kids love – pizza, ice cream and cookies. There are charades and talent shows and star searches for older children.

The main advantage children see in a cruise? They don't have their parents continuously hovering over them making sure they are okay. If you have brought children along, it could be hours before you see them again because they will be too busy having fun at the various shipboard facilities.

The trend of children traveling on cruise ships is growing. More than 15 per cent of adult passengers on North American based cruises bring along their children. Some cruise lines have responded with special programs and counselors who plan fun events for the various age groups.

A cruise is one of the best types of vacations on which you can take children. They are kept so busy and entertained, it's not unusual for those who have been on a vacation that combined a trip to Florida's Disney World with a Caribbean cruise to say it's a toss-up which was more fun! If you have kids, a cruise is a great vacation for the entire family.

Romance

The image of cruising is suffused with romance. Books, films and television all reinforce the notion that cruise ships are conducive to amorous feelings. Cruise lines, of course, nurture this aspect of ship travel. Couples celebrating an anniversary or renewing their vows will often receive, compliments of the hotel manager, a bottle of champagne or a specially baked cake. Honeymooners are given the royal treatment on board a ship, often being invited to a private Captain's cocktail party or receiving a special bottle of bubbly in their cabin. Some cruise lines can actually marry couples on board during the cruise. But apart from any special touches provided by the cruise line, the general ambiance of a cruise ship is ideal for a romantic interlude.

Strolling the decks together under a starlit sky, watching the sun set as you linger at the ship's rail, ordering breakfast in bed each morning, sharing an intimate table for two in the dining room each evening, lingering in a cozy corner of your favorite bar – there's no end to the romantic moments a couple can share on board a cruise ship.

Shipboard Security and Sense of Community

There is, on board a ship, a feeling of community and security that is hard to duplicate on land. A cruise is a unique experience; most passengers board the same day and are able to wander at ease throughout their floating resort and share common experiences with fellow travelers. Passengers do not hesitate to smile, say hello, and even share an impromptu joke with one another.

In urban settings, people generally remain somewhat wary of strangers. However, because a ship remains off limits to the public, its sense of sanctuary is distinct and reassuring. Passengers, crew and authorized shore personnel are the only ones allowed access and, upon boarding a ship, people soon lower their guard and usually raise their standards of politeness in keeping with proper shipboard etiquette.

On most ships, the captain and hotel manager set the standard of gracious behavior, warmly greeting every passenger attending the gala welcoming party. Their demeanor is reflected in the hotel staff who pamper passengers with friendly and courteous service. The atmosphere this creates is not stilted or stuffy, but one of genuine cheerfulness and common courtesy. Only a confirmed boor would misbehave in such a genteel atmosphere, for it is simply too much the way we would always like to be treated.

Security on board a ship is unobtrusive. After initial embarkation, at which time passengers and their luggage go through standard security checks, you present an identification card (issued to you at the beginning of the cruise) when re-embarking at each port of call. The ship's security officer is often positioned at the gangway, but this screening is conducted in a very low-key manner.

Perhaps one of the most appealing aspects of cruising, especially for women, is being able to wander throughout the ship's public areas at any time, day or night, and not be worried about personal safety. With approximately one crew member for every two or three passengers, there are always staff on hand to lend assistance in any type of situation. And women on their own can feel totally at ease in the ship's bars, nightclubs and casino, secure in the knowledge that anyone they meet is a fellow passenger.

This feeling of security extends to parents traveling with children. They can let their older ones wander off to the playroom without worrying that they will become lost or frightened. And children welcome the novelty of being independent of their parents as each age group pursues its own organized activities.

Friendships that develop on a cruise are often fleeting but some do endure. New friends are easily made in this pampered and relaxed atmosphere, whether it be a fellow 'regular' at your favorite bar or the engaging couple you share a dinner table with each evening. On the last night of a cruise it's not unusual to see fellow passengers hugging one another good-bye and exchanging addresses. Whether or not they ever see each other again, passengers often say that the people they met on board were an important factor in their enjoyment of the cruise.

Passengers on a river vessel also enjoy a sociable atmosphere, for they share an interest in the history and culture of the area they have chosen to visit and this makes for easy conversation in the restaurant, bar and observation lounge. With scenery passing close by your vessel, a river cruise might be compared to a train journey at a fraction of the speed, with plenty of time to comment on the moving pageant.

Reliability of a Cruise Holiday

One of the great appeals of a cruise is knowing the consistency of what you are purchasing. If you discover a cruise line to your liking, you can cruise anywhere – be it the Caribbean or Alaska – and be assured of the same level of food and service again and again.

At first glance the cruise industry appears to be a complexity of different ships and itineraries. There is a wide selection among the ships for level of service, facilities and cuisine but there is conformity in many other aspects. In true naval tradition, the cruise industry is highly regulated and maintains stringent standards out of a sense of pride as much as good business.

Cruise ships have weekly safety drills for crew and officers. In addition, if the ship sails from a US port, regular sanitation inspections by the US Public Health Department and US Coast Guard ensure high standards of hygiene and fire prevention on all cruise ships.

The ships are also annually rated by cruise experts and listed in various publications providing travel agents with current information on specifications and level of quality for each ship. This allows your travel agent to recommend a particular cruise line or cruise ship with confidence in its fulfilling a pre-established level of accommodation, service, cuisine and other on-board amenities.

As a result, unpleasant surprises are rare for the consumer. You can learn from your agent exactly what facilities your ship of choice contains, the level of service to expect, the nationality of the officers and hotel staff, and the atmosphere (i.e. casual, semi-formal, formal) of the ship. Your agent can also tell you the exact size, lay-out and location of your cabin.

One of the main reasons the cruise industry has enjoyed such phenomenal success is its reputation for serving fine cuisine. Cruise lines servicing the North American market generally offer continental cuisine, sometimes modified for a particular locale (i.e. Pacific salmon in Alaska). The better the cruise line, the wider the range of cuisine, but even popular-priced ships maintain a high level of food service. Passengers with diverse culinary tastes can choose from a tantalizing selection of dishes. Meal offerings, in addition to breakfast, lunch and dinner, often extend to afternoon tea, poolside barbecues and midnight buffets – and there is always room service.

Standards of cleanliness on board ship are keenly pursued. These high standards extend from the galley to the entire passenger area of the ship. Your cabin steward will clean your stateroom twice a day and is always nearby to attend to any additional requests. The public areas are also kept spotless, with tables promptly cleared, the decks scrubbed, and the brass polished.

Last but not least, the ships' itineraries are established well in advance and are described in detail so that you know what ports of call are included in a particular cruise, as well as the time of arrival and departure at each destination, and which days are spent at sea. This allows you to plan your vacation long before you board the ship.

Variety of Shipboard Facilities

The refined elegance of yesteryear is still evident in grand foyers and spacious dining rooms, but gone are the segregated public areas and three classes of passengers. Today, everyone cruises first-class (with the exception of the *QE2* which has three levels of dining room service, depending on the grade of cabin booked) and all passengers enjoy the on-board amenities for which modern ships have been described as floating resorts.

The upper decks of cruise ships provide the open areas for sports and leisure activities. Here you can stroll, jog, or recline in a deck chair with a view of far horizons. Standard features on newer ships now include at least one swimming pool, if not two or three. One is often located out of doors and another one is either enclosed or covered by a plexiglass roof that opens and closes, depending on the weather conditions. A whirlpool is usually located nearby, as well as a wading pool for youngsters.

The upper decks are also where passengers will find a jogging track, a games court, and possibly a golf putting green or net-enclosed driving range. (Royal Caribbean Cruise Line's *Legend of the Seas* was the first ship to include an 18-hole golf course on its top 'Compass Deck'.)

A ship's gymnasium is another popular sports facility, with its exercise equipment and fitness instructors on hand. Ships often have a health or beauty spa, with sauna and steam room, where you can enjoy a relaxing massage. Many ships have a full-length or wrap-around promenade deck, which is excellent for those who enjoy long walks. Some newer ships use a soft rubber compound on the promenade deck and others stay with the traditional teak – which is lovely to look at as well as walk on.

For passengers seeking to improve their minds as well as their bodies, the ship's library will likely contain a good selection of reference material and bestselling paperbacks. A card/games room is often part of or adjacent to the library. It is not uncommon to see the tables in this room filled with animated card players who, just a few days earlier, were complete strangers.

Cruise ships also have an area set aside for shops and boutiques selling designer jewelry, perfume and clothes, as well as a selection of liquor, all at duty-free prices. Basic toiletries can also be purchased on board, in case you forgot to pack your toothbrush or razor. Film, cigarettes and books can generally be found in the shops.

On-board services usually include a launderette (with iron and ironing board) as well as a dry cleaner. At the photo shop you can purchase prints taken of you and your cruise companions by one of the ship's photographers. You can also have your own print film developed on board. The ship's doctor and nurse can be consulted at the medical center, and a number of ships provide a playroom and babysitting services.

Most modern ships also pride themselves on a range of entertainment that rivals many small cities. Included are a cinema, a casino, a show lounge where musicals and cabaret revues are staged each evening, and nightclubs with musical entertainment ranging from disco to classical. You can watch television in the privacy of your cabin, the channel selection including recently-released movies, travel documentaries, and on-board events taking place in the ship's show lounge. Some cruise lines have their own satellite hook-up to bring passengers an all-news network.

Range of Activities

Although there are dozens of shipboard activities – both group and individual – passengers are free to participate as much or as little as they like. You can do whatever you want and if that means taking a nap while the rest of the world is playing volleyball, that's your prerogative. There is absolutely no pressure placed on anyone to join in any activities taking place on board the ship (except the mandatory lifeboat drill) and it's quite easy for passengers to find a quiet spot in a lounge or an empty deck chair to watch the scenery, read a good book, or engage in conversation. The pace you choose to pursue is entirely under your control.

That said, it should also be noted that the ocean liner days of pipe-smoking gents and long-skirted ladies playing a genteel game of shuffleboard have given way to contemporary activities that were unthinkable a hundred years ago. In daytime, show lounges and gyms are used by casually clad passengers stretching, bouncing and puffing to the urgings of an aerobics instructor. Fitness programs have become a standard feature on many modern ships and they include hydro calisthenics and work-outs on

A new day, a new port.
Above – Fort-de-France,
Martinique
Opposite – St George
Harbour, Bermuda
Below – Charlotte Amalie,
St Thomas

Top – A Caribbean sunset enjoyed at the ship's rail.
Middle – Vigie Beach, St Lucia
Bottom – Glacier Bay, Alaska

Day and night, there are many opportunities to share a relaxing, romantic moment on a cruise vacation. Whether enjoying a glass of champagne on a moonlit night, or a gourmet meal before a stage show, romance and cruising are a natural combination.

Some of the world's most memorable sights, such as the Panama Canal (above) and Alaska's Misty Fjords (below), are best seen from the deck of a cruise ship.

computerized exercise equipment.

Jogging usually takes place on the sports deck, leaving the promenade deck to those who prefer walking, strolling, or simply leaning on the ship's rail with a drink in hand. Basketball, volleyball and table tennis tournaments are arranged by the cruise director's staff, as are skeet shooting, deck football and cricket. And, yes, you can still get in a game of shuffleboard.

All this non-stop physical activity may sound a bit exhausting but there are more leisurely pursuits to be found. Chess, checkers, crafts sessions, fashion shows, and card games are all part of most cruises. People looking to pamper themselves (and willing to pay for personal services) can indulge in a massage, facial and new hair-style in the ship's beauty spa and salon.

On days when the ship is at sea there are a number of activities taking place simultaneously, including lectures on the upcoming ports of call and the shore excursions being offered at each destination. These lectures are replayed throughout the day on one of the channels featured on your cabin's television, if your cabin contains this amenity. Films are aired on cabin televisions as well as in the ship's cinema, and each day's movie schedule is posted in the daily newsletter that is slipped under your door.

The daily program keeps you informed of all activities planned for that day, including religious services, and it soon becomes apparent that no passenger could participate in every event unless they stayed on board for a few months and tried new activities every day. Of course, organized activities are not for everyone, and simply enjoying the ambiance of the ship and the passing scenery fills the days for many travelers.

Whether at sea or at port, you make of the day whatever you wish. The same holds true for the night. You can take in the stage show, enjoying musicals and cabaret revues which feature talented comedians, singers, jugglers and magicians. If you're in a mellow mood, you can enjoy after-dinner drinks to the melodious sounds of a string quartet, or settle into a comfortable seat of a piano bar. Dancing – everything from ballroom to disco – can be enjoyed in several of the ship's lounges, and gentlemen hosts are often on board to serve as dance partners for single women. Karaoke singing is often featured in one of the ship's bars.

The pings and bells of the casino slot machines is the sound of music for some, and most cruise lines oblige with a full range of gaming opportunities. Blackjack lessons are usually available.

Passengers soon learn where the busy areas of a ship are at certain times of the day, where the quiet areas are, and everyone gravitates to the area and activity that appeals to them.

Opportunity to Pursue a Special Interest

A number of cruise lines now offer special cruises featuring guest hosts who are experts in a particular field. Their talks, clinics, performances and hosted tours ashore cover interests as diverse as bridge and bird watching, golf and gardening. Photography buffs can learn helpful tips from the professionals and bridge players can book onto special cruises that feature qualified professionals.

Country music cruises are popular, as are jazz festivals at sea, which feature celebrity-hosted concerts and acclaimed musicians. Dance enthusiasts will be tempted to book onto Big Band cruises that feature the sounds of swing.

River cruises are noted for their knowledgeable hosts – experts in their academic fields – who provide passengers with fascinating historical and cultural background on the lands they are cruising past and the ports of call. One of the best examples of this is a journey along the Nile where excursions to view the great pyramids and temples of Ancient Egypt are part of the cruise package.

The Chance to Visit Many Destinations

People often choose a cruise based on the destinations included in the itinerary. Cruising offers them the opportunity to visit a variety of countries and capitals without ever changing hotels. Not only are they saved the bother of packing and unpacking as they travel from one destination to another, they do not have to deal with foreign and fluctuating currencies, except for incidental expenses incurred on shore, such as shopping purchases or cab rides. Clearing each country's customs and immigration department is another hurdle that is handled by the ship's staff, with the entire passenger list quickly cleared with authorities immediately upon the ship's docking. Also, cruise ships do much of their steaming at night while the passengers sleep, so precious vacation time is well utilized.

Many who travel by ship say that nothing compares with a seaborne arrival. Whether it's watching the sun rise above a tropical island as your ship approaches its lush shores or seeing the sights of a bustling harbourfront draw ever closer, arriving by sea is a travel experience of unparalleled romance and timelessness.

The early risers will be out on deck to watch their ship pull into port. With courtesy flags raised, the ship sidles up to the dock where shore workers with heavy eyes wait for the crew to toss the docking lines. Once again the ship is linked to land, her passengers eager to disembark and explore a new destination.

Many of the world's great cities were built beside oceans and rivers, and their universal appeal – both as centers of commerce and as tourist meccas – often translates into high prices for hotels and restaurant meals. Yet people traveling by ship needn't be concerned, for their floating hotel will take them to some of the world's most expensive cities for a fraction of what it would cost if they were staying on shore.

Cruise ships and river vessels take advantage of centuries-old transportation routes, and their passengers travel at a relaxed pace which allows them to absorb the unfolding sights and sounds of the landscapes they are gliding past. A cruise along the Rhine or the Nile is a journey through history and one that everyone can re-live as their vessel plies ancient waterways once used by civilizations far removed from the automobiles and airplanes of the 20th century. And when a cruise ship moors at an exotic island, its passengers can experience the exhilaration felt by seafarers of the past who looked with anticipation to landing at these fragrant and fabled shores.

A day in port is an ideal way for travelers to take a good look at a new place with a view to returning at a later date for a longer stay. This sampling of ports is a favorite pastime of cruise passengers who enjoy sharing and comparing their impressions when they return to the ship at the end of the day.

Frequent cruisers tend to be well traveled and interested in a wide range of vacations. They look upon a cruise as not only a complete holiday in itself, but also as an opportunity to check out unfamiliar destinations before deciding to book, at some point in the future, a land-based holiday at a particular location.

Variety of Destinations and Types of Cruises

Cruises now cover virtually every travel region of the world. Whether it's the ever-popular cruising grounds of the Caribbean and Mediterranean, the remote shores of Alaska and the South Pacific, or the great rivers that meander across continents, where there's water there are cruise vessels.

The choice of itineraries and cruises is now so extensive, an experienced travel agent will save most consumers a great deal of time when choosing a cruise vacation that will satisfy their interests, tastes and expectations.

The Caribbean remains the most popular cruising area in the world, and for good reason. Over two and half million cruise visitors each year come to see the islands of this turquoise blue sea. The Caribbean offers beautiful beaches, sunny weather, and historic ports of call where one can enjoy a unique cultural blend of European colonialism and African heritage.

The Mediterranean is another region that offers cruise visitors a taste of foreign cultures and the opportunity to see some of the world's most famous historical sites – all this against a backdrop of beaches and blue skies. The sunny Med is second only to the Caribbean in terms of popularity.

Quite different in appeal is the rugged grandeur of Alaska, where massive tidewater glaciers and marine mammals such as whales, dolphins and sea otters can be seen from the ship. The Far East is also enticing cruise passengers in ever increasing numbers, while the fjords of Scandinavia remain for many one of the most breathtaking areas to visit by cruise ship.

Whether visiting the famous port cities of the Baltic Sea, transiting the Panama Canal, or succumbing to the lure of the South Pacific, the choice of sea port destinations is eclectic. And where the ocean ends, river vessels take over, threading their way along such historic and scenic routes as the Rhine, Main and Danube Rivers of Europe, the Nile of Egypt, and America's Mississippi and Columbia.

Another way to see more of a region is to extend an ocean cruise with an overland tour, such as Alaska's land packages which can include plying the Yukon River on board a paddlewheeler or taking a private railcar to Denali National Park to view North America's highest peak – Mount McKinley. Another overland tour for passengers taking an Alaska cruise out of Vancouver, is a coach tour or rail journey to the Canadian Rockies, location of Banff and Jasper National Parks, famous worldwide for their alpine splendor.

A Mediterranean cruise vacation can be extended by boarding the Orient Express in Venice and travelling across Europe by rail. A Caribbean cruise can include a pre or post-land tour of Florida's major attractions and miles of white beaches. Cruise travelers to the Far East often disembark for tours to Beijing and the Great Wall, and those cruising Australia frequently include an overland trip to the Outback.

Potential cruisers must ask themselves not only where they want to go cruising, but on what type of cruise, what style of ship, and what length of cruise. There is tremendous variety in cruise duration – everything from three-day cruises in the Bahamas to round-the-world cruises of 100 or more days. However, the two main choices are *loop cruises* that begin and end at the same port, and are usually of one- to two-weeks in length, and *line cruises* that begin at one port and end at another after calling at various ports in between. *Repositioning cruises* are offered on board ships that are moving from one cruising area to another at the end of a season, an example being a springtime cruise from the Caribbean to Alaska which includes a transit of the Panama Canal and ports of call along the Mexican Riviera and California.

The range of ships is as impressive as the wide open sea. Classic ocean liners, such as the *Queen Elizabeth 2*, are joined today by an ever-growing list of modern ships built specifically for cruise vacations. These include

Fitness-conscious passengers can work out daily in the health spa/gymnasium found on board modern cruise ships.

the modern liners built during the '80s and today's megaships, which hold up to 2,000 passengers and provide recreational facilities that rival land-based resorts. But large ships are not the only choices awaiting the cruise consumer. Many prefer the specialized cruise vessels, which offer a different type of cruise experience.

Expedition ships are smaller and sometimes designed tougher to withstand big seas and the occasional brush with ice as they venture into the higher latitudes. Tall ships are popular with vacationers seeking some 'soft adventure' while visiting tropical shores. Also of special appeal are the small luxury ships which take their passengers off the beaten track to a cruising area's smaller and quieter ports.

The Caribbean, for example, can be enjoyed on any type of ship – from the dazzling new megaships to the small sailing ships that anchor off secluded beaches for picnic lunches. The Mediterranean is also serviced by a complete range of cruise vessels – from modern luxury liners to intimate yacht-like ships – with passengers disembarking at sun-drenched islands and historic ports to view ancient ruins and man-made wonders. And Alaska's lofty scenery can be seen both from the decks of a large cruise ship or amid the casual atmosphere of an expedition vessel carrying less than 200 passengers.

In choosing a ship, it must also be noted that each has its own atmosphere in terms of nationality of the passengers and crew; the degree of formality or casualness; its specific appeal to singles, families or couples; and its emphasis on certain activities and interests.

Shore Excursions

As comfortable and enjoyable as being on a ship is, going ashore at each new port is an important aspect of cruising. Shoreside activities include sightseeing, shopping, adventure tours such as submarine rides and flight-seeing trips, and recreational pursuits such as golf and sportfishing. Most cruise lines offer organized shore excursions for the convenience of their passengers and these are usually described in a booklet that is enclosed with your cruise tickets as well as at on-board presentations given by the ship's shore excursion manager. There is a charge for such excursions but they are usually fairly priced and the tour operators used are reliable and monitored by the cruise company to ensure they maintain the level of service promised to their passengers, with the added advantage that the ship will wait for any of its overdue excursions.

However, independent-minded passengers need not feel that pre-booked shore excursions are their only option when exploring various ports of call. Choices include renting a car, hiring a cab, using the public transport system or simply setting off on foot to explore the town and outlying area. With a bit of preparatory reading and a reliable map in hand, a person can see and do a great deal in the time available.

The locale determines the nature of shoreside activities available to cruise passengers. In the Caribbean, for instance, many of the 'shore' activities actually take place in the water – swimming off beaches, snorkeling among coral reefs, scuba diving to shipwrecks now inhabited by tropical fish, and skimming across the water on a windsurfer, catamaran or 12-metre racing yacht. For those who prefer to stay dry, submarine rides and glass bottom boats afford effortless views of the colorful underwater world.

Airborne excursions include helicopter and seaplane flights for panoramic views of coral atolls and the lush vegetation of island interiors. There are also boat trips to beautiful, secluded beaches and river rafting expeditions through tropical rainforests where waterfalls and freshwater pools create a Garden of Eden setting for the exotic birds, plants and animals living there.

In addition to the Caribbean's natural beauty, its colonial history can be explored on island drives to such points of interest as Nelson's Dockyard on Antigua, Drake's Seat on St. Thomas, and the imposing fortress of El Morro at San Juan, Puerto Rico. Many of the former plantation estates are open to the public, their grand mansions now museums and the grounds now parkland containing picnic tables and botanical gardens. And of course there are the port cities, where European colonial architecture is reflected in government buildings and grand hotels, and where narrow cobblestone streets are lined with inviting shops and restaurants.

The Mediterranean also offers an appealing combination of beautiful beaches, historic sites and cosmopolitan ports of call where visitors can experience exotic cultures and cuisine. Organized shore excursions are usually coach tours to ancient ruins and temples, monasteries and cathedrals, museums and art galleries, or perhaps a drive into the hills, past cyprus groves, olive orchards and vineyards, to visit some of the local villages.

Other Med excursions involve boarding a smaller cruise vessel that takes you to nearby islands to enjoy their coastal scenery, including craggy coves and beach-lined bays. For those who prefer to stroll the streets and browse in the local shops, a day in port can soon slip by. Another popular pastime is to simply while away the day at the beach – sunbathing, swimming and gazing out to sea from the shade of a beach umbrella, a cool refreshment in hand.

Alaska has some of the most developed and diverse shore excursions of any cruising area. Most people travel to Alaska to see its famed wilderness, which is why sidetrips to glaciers, fjords and mountain lakes are extremely popular. Floatplanes and helicopters whisk passengers over glacier-filled valleys and rugged mountains. They fly low enough for passengers to see mountain goats and other wildlife such as beachcombing bears. More wildlife – especially whales and sea otters – can also be spotted on boating and kayaking excursions.

CHAPTER TWO

TODAY'S CRUISING CHOICES

Worldwide Destinations, Types of Cruises, Variety of Ships

There's no longer such a thing as a typical cruise. With cruise vacations steadily increasing in popularity, the selection of cruises is also increasing. Today there's a cruise package that appeals to every type of traveler, and the variety of ships now servicing the world's cruising regions is unprecedented. The choices for customers are limited only by each passenger's personal preference.

WHERE TO GO?

The world is broken into cruising regions by the cruise lines. These boundaries sometimes overlap and longer cruises often encompass a number of regions. Nonetheless, the major cruise areas are the Caribbean, the Mediterranean, Alaska, trans-Panama Canal, Mexican Riviera, Europe, Bermuda (and Eastern Seaboard), Trans-Atlantic, the South Pacific, and Hawaii. Adventure destinations, such as Antarctica and the Amazon, are also beginning to appear on itineraries.

The Caribbean ranks first as a cruise destination, annually attracting almost 50 per cent of total cruisers, followed by the Mediterranean and Alaska. Europe, the Far East and Southeast Asia are fast becoming popular destinations as passengers discover that cruise ships provide unique accessibility to large, popular and expensive cities.

River cruises are a specialized type of cruise and are gaining wide attention with both new and veteran cruisers. Many of the world's rivers are open to cruises and include a range of experience from that of the ancient Nile to the historic rivers of Europe, such as the Rhine and the Danube. Famous American rivers like the Mississippi, the Ohio and the Columbia provide a unique perspective on America's sprawling landscape and frontier heritage. China's Yangtze, South America's Amazon, Ireland's Shannon, and Canada's St Lawrence are also traversed by cruise vessels.

The type of cruise ship you choose will of course color your perceptions of any cruise area, but there are universal attractions to each region. The following is an overview of each major cruise area. *For more detail regarding ports of call, please see Chapter 4.*

The Caribbean (including Bahamas)

The Caribbean has long appealed to travelers yearning to escape the grip of winter for a week or two of sunshine and sandy beaches. And with dozens of islands to visit, a person could cruise to the Caribbean many times and still find reasons to return.

During the peak cruising season (mid-December to mid-April) some ports of call are inundated with visitors, but the Caribbean Sea is a vast body of water and the many ships plying its warm waters can spread out, offering various routes and combinations of ports. The cruise lines are well aware it is the Caribbean's diversity that makes it such an appealing vacation destination and so arrange their itineraries to give passengers the best of everything. Careful research and planning goes into choosing ports of call, examples being: San Juan for Spanish history and nightlife; St Maarten for Dutch culture / St Martin for French; St Thomas for duty free shopping; St Lucia for lush, mountainous scenery; and Barbados for British heritage.

Of course it's the natural beauty of these tropical islands, their beach-ringed shores lapped by a turquoise sea, that draws visitors from colder climes. In fact, some cruise ships anchor off private, undeveloped islands and treat their passengers to a day spent in a classic tropical-island setting. With almost no tidal range in the Caribbean, its waters remain clear and warm year round – ideal conditions for swimming, snorkeling and other watersports.

The West Indies extend in a wide, 2,500-mile arc from Florida to Venezuela, separating the Atlantic Ocean from the Caribbean Sea. Because of its extensive size, the Caribbean has been divided into service areas by the cruise lines. They use a variety of base ports, the major ones being Florida's Miami and Fort Lauderdale, and Puerto Rico's San Juan.

The Western Caribbean includes such destinations as Jamaica, Grand Cayman and the Mexican ports of Playa del Carmen and Cozumel. An

Eastern Caribbean cruise might take in the Bahamas, San Juan and the Virgin Islands. Southern Caribbean cruises sail to the Leeward and Windward groups of the Lesser Antilles as well as islands like Barbados, Aruba, Curacao, and the South American ports of La Guaira (Caracas) and Cartagena.

Caribbean cruises generally range from one to two weeks in duration, depending on the area covered, and some itineraries include a partial transit of the Panama Canal. Short three- or four-day cruises out of Miami to the Bahamas and from San Juan to the US Virgin Islands are also popular. English is widely spoken throughout the Caribbean and the US dollar is the common currency.

Mediterranean

If you are intrigued by the ancient worlds of Greece, Rome, Byzantium and Egypt, there is no better way to explore these regions than a cruise to the Mediterranean. Thoroughly diverse in both ancient and modern cultures, the Mediterranean offers dozens of foreign ports located on three different continents. The world's largest inland sea, the Mediterranean is surrounded by Europe, Asia and Africa. Its coastal regions and islands, graced with fine beaches, offer visitors a climate that is warm and dry with an abundance of sunshine.

The fall season is the most popular time of year for cruising this 'sea in the midst of lands' but cruise ships ply these tidal-free waters all summer long, starting in April or May. The Mediterranean's mountainous shores, formed over time by earthquakes and volcanic disturbances, are comprised of capes and headlands where clifftop towns and ancient ruins now stand.

The varying itineraries offered by cruise lines are a study in history, art and culture. Rome, Florence and Venice contain some of the world's most prized Renaissance art and architecture, and at Istanbul – formerly Constantinople – masterpieces of Byzantine architecture can be viewed. The Hellenic times of Ancient Greece can be revisited on a cruise that stops at Athens to view the Parthenon atop the Acropolis, the island of Rhodes – a center of learning in the 3rd century BC – and the ancient island of Crete, where an advanced civilization flourished as long ago as 3000 BC. Whatever the period of interest, there are suitable ports of call to fascinate the history buff.

The Mediterranean's ancient ruins, medieval architecture and Renaissance art are found in a setting of outstanding natural beauty – terraced orchards and vineyards grace the hillsides, and white beaches rim the shorelines. The sea itself contains some 400 species of fish, and the sponge and coral life is plentiful. Travelers wishing to sample the

Mediterranean's modern cultures can stroll through bazaars and linger at sidewalk cafes while sampling local wines and drinking in the surrounding ambiance at each port of call.

Alaska

Spectacular scenery and abundant wildlife are the main attractions of Alaska cruises, which run from early May to late September. The home port for Alaskan cruising is Vancouver, Canada, located at the southern end of the Inside Passage – a long, protected stretch of water containing hundreds of forested islands, winding channels and mountain fjords. The best vantage point on an Alaska cruise is the ship's rail, where you can view hanging waterfalls cascading hundreds of feet into emerald green waters, and tidewater glaciers dropping large chunks of blue ice straight into the sea.

The chance to spot a whale or dolphin adds an additional element of excitement, especially when someone in the dining room shouts "Whale!" and people abandon their gourmet meals to rush to the windows. Ports of call are also rich in wilderness. Eagles perch on hydro poles and local flight-seeing trips whisk passengers over mountains and valleys still blanketed by glaciers that formed during the last Ice Age. At lower elevations, the mild maritime climate has produced lush forests of spruce, hemlock and cedar, from which the native Indians carve their monumental totem poles.

An Inside Passage cruise to Alaska begins and ends in Vancouver, while cruises that include the Gulf of Alaska in their itinerary operate one-way routes between Vancouver and Anchorage – Alaska's largest city with a population of approximately a quarter of a million. These straight-line cruises are referred to as the 'Glacier Route' because they include some of Alaska's most impressive tidewater glaciers, namely Hubbard Glacier in Yakutat Bay and Columbia Glacier in Prince William Sound. Both cruises stop at various ports, such as Ketchikan, Juneau and Sitka, along the Inside Passage.

Panama Canal

Most seasoned cruisers will agree that transiting the Panama Canal is something everyone should do at least once in their lifetime. One of the world's great engineering feats, the Panama Canal is a 51-mile-long ditch that was built by the US military to bisect the Isthmus of Panama and thus provide a convenient shipping route between the Atlantic Ocean (via the Caribbean Sea) and the Pacific Ocean. The canal is now a popular itinerary for cruise ships, which regularly transit its six locks and two lakes.

A ship prepares to enter the next set of locks during a trans-Panama Canal cruise.

Each spring and fall, a fleet of ships traveling between the Caribbean and Alaska offer repositioning cruises which include a transit of the Panama Canal. Other ships offer trans-canal cruises throughout the winter cruise season. A trans-canal cruise can vary in length from seven to 17 days. Itineraries range from a partial transit of the canal to cruises that include Mexico's Pacific coast and islands of the Caribbean.

Mexican Riviera

The golden beaches of Mexico's Pacific coast attract vacationers throughout the year, but October through May are the most popular months for cruising. Dubbed the Mexican Riviera, this 2,000-mile-long coast of rocky headlands and secluded beaches is famous for its rugged beauty and bustling resorts.

A number of cruise lines incorporate the Mexican Riviera in their Panama Canal cruises, while others devote entire five- to 10-day itineraries to various ports of call situated along this unique stretch of ocean coast. Most popular is Acapulco, a resort city situated on a beautiful bay backed by mountains and filled with luxury hotels and private villas, including one at which John and Jackie Kennedy spent their honeymoon.

The Fjords of Norway

Scandinavia continues to draw visitors each summer. Towering peaks, green mountain valleys, fishing villages nestled at the head of river-fed fjords – this land of endless summer days is breathtaking. Its grandeur inspired Edvard Grieg, the 'Voice of Norway', to compose his stirring piano concertos and set the words of Norwegian poets to music. Less than four per cent of Norway's rugged land is cultivated; its vast mountain pastures are used for grazing cattle and sheep and, in the north, for raising reindeer.

A Scandinavian cruise also includes the neighboring countries of Denmark and Sweden. Denmark's cosmopolitan capital of Copenhagen contains the famous Tivoli Gardens. Nearby is Elsinore Castle, the setting of Shakespeare's Hamlet. The Swedish capital of Stockholm, situated on several peninsulas and islands, always fascinates visitors with its Royal Palace and medieval quarter, where winding lanes and arches lead to restaurants housed in cellars.

Baltic ports of call include Helsinki (capital of Finland) and St. Petersburg, where the Czars of Russia once ruled from the Winter Palace and where the Hermitage Museum contains some of the world's greatest works of art.

Bermuda

Lying some 570 miles off the coast of North Carolina, Bermuda is a bit of 'Olde England' in a semi-tropical setting. Spanish mariners were likely the first explorers to stumble across Bermuda in the 16th century, but the islands remained uninhabited until some British colonists bound for Virginia were shipwrecked here in 1609. Bermuda remains a British crown colony, and thirsty visitors can order a pint in one of the authentic English pubs or watch a local cricket match.

With its fragrant flowers, warm weather, pink coral beaches and pastel-colored homes, Bermuda pleases all the senses. Noel Coward and Mark Twain both wrote effusively about Bermuda's refined beauty – all of it contained in an area covering just 21 square miles. Only two miles across at its widest point, Bermuda has over 100 beaches and, with eight golf courses, the most golf per acre of any country in the world.

From May through October a limited number of cruise lines offer one-week round-trip cruises from New York or Boston. During an average four-day stay at Bermuda, the ship serves as a floating hotel while its passengers tour this enchanting chain of British-flavored islands.

North America's Eastern Seaboard

Originally colonized by European settlers, the Atlantic coastlines of Canada and the US are being discovered anew by shipboard passengers who can enjoy splendid scenery combined with old world charm. The region's enduring architecture, regional dialects and local customs all reflect its deep-rooted ties to Europe which hark back to the 16th century and the arrival of Spanish, French, British and Dutch explorers.

Summer and fall are the prime seasons for cruising this region of fishing harbors and clapboard houses, Cape Cod mansions and clam chowder soup. Fall foliage cruises are especially popular, when autumn's blaze of color turns leafy lanes into perfect settings for Norman Rockwell paintings. Specific areas covered by various one- to two-week cruises include the St. Lawrence River, Canada's Atlantic provinces and the American states of New England.

Trans-Atlantic

Before the advent of jet travel, the North Atlantic served as a conveyor belt for ships delivering passengers between Europe and North America. These passengers ranged from the rich and famous who sailed in luxury with servants, lap dogs and trunks of clothes, to immigrants who could afford only the basic accommodations of steerage class.

Until the mid-1960s it was cheaper to cross the Atlantic by ship than by plane; however, the introduction of jumbo jets in the early 1970s changed all that. Today, only one major superliner offers regular transatlantic service – the *Queen Elizabeth 2*. The fastest and most famous cruise ship in the world, Cunard's *QE2* embarks on approximately two dozen annual sailings between Southampton and New York. On a typical crossing, passengers spend five nights on board

Some people still book passage on the *QE2* when they are moving across the Atlantic and, in addition to a generous baggage allowance, the *QE2* can transport cars and accommodate pets in its kennel.

Other cruise lines offer seasonal transatlantic crossings – each spring and fall – when some of their ships travel between the Caribbean and Europe.

Hawaii/South Pacific

Most world travelers dream of one day visiting the far-flung islands of the South Pacific. Ever since the fragrant beauty of Tahiti inspired a mutiny among the *Bounty's* crew, people have been drawn to the south seas to see what all the fuss was about. Over the years, writers, painters and hedonists have all made the pilgrimage, first arriving by ship, then by jet plane, and now, once again, by ship.

Today cruise lines offer exotic sea voyages to these lagoon-fringed islands of hibiscus and coconut palms. One memorable landfall after another awaits passengers who board a cruise ship bound for the turquoise waters of the South Pacific. San Francisco and Los Angeles are the main ports for these paradise-bound ships, and Hawaii is often the first port of call.

A full cruise of the Pacific, which may also include Australia, New Zealand, Southeast Asia and the Far East, will take 30 to 80 days depending on the itinerary. However, two- to three-week segments of these 'grand voyages' can also be booked, with passengers flying to a port of embarkation and flying home from their port of disembarkation. For example, a person could board a ship in Los Angeles or San Francisco for a 20-day cruise to Sydney, Australia and return by air.

The Far East

Shrouded in mystery and ancient rituals, the Far East is slowly opening its doors to tourism, and visitors can now peek inside temples and palaces where philosophers and emperors of ancient dynasties once resided. Hong Kong has long welcomed foreigners and today this free port is the hub of trade, banking and shopping for the Far East. It is also a popular port of call with cruise passengers who enjoy the vibrant pace of this British colony. Hong Kong is promoted by both local and Chinese tourism officials as a cruise destination that will continue to welcome visitors long after Great Britain's lease expires in 1997.

The exotic ports of Southeast Asia are also attracting cruise visitors, places such as the mystical island of Bali, the bustling port of Singapore, and the kingdom of Thailand. Another popular cruise destination is Japan, a modernized nation of skyscrapers, shops and restaurants, but also one of Shinto temples, meditative shrines and bonsai gardens.

Passengers can fly to a local port of Southeast Asia or the Far East and embark on a one- to four-week cruise of the area.

Atlantic Isles

The Canary Islands, which lie in the Atlantic Ocean off Africa's Spanish Sahara, once attracted pirates and privateers (Sir Francis Drake among them) to their beach-lined shores. Today these rugged islands, volcanic in origin, are a year-round holiday destination offering visitors a sub-tropical climate and Spanish flavor.

The Madeira Islands, lying 350 miles off Morocco, are also popular with cruise passengers. Their unusual scenic beauty, which so captivated

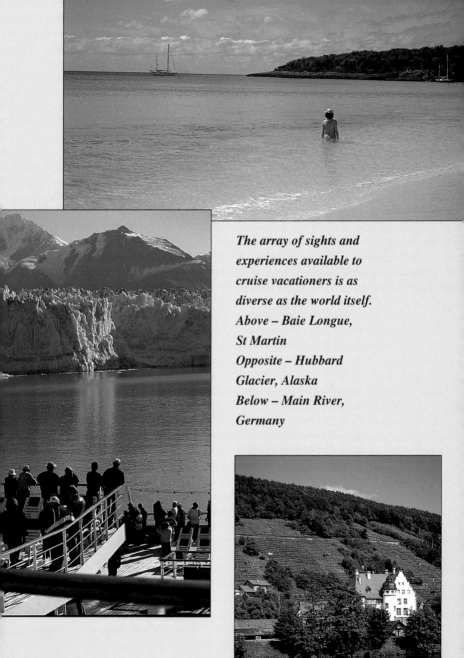

The array of sights and experiences available to cruise vacationers is as diverse as the world itself.
Above – Baie Longue, St Martin
Opposite – Hubbard Glacier, Alaska
Below – Main River, Germany

Top – Seabourn Legend, a luxury small ship, docks at St Lucia
Above – Wind Song, a sailing ship, cruises French Polynesia
Left – Spirit of Alaska, an expedition ship, plies the pristine waters of Canada's Inside Passage.

The different types of ships offering cruise vacations include classic liners like the QE2 (above) and modern megaships such as Legend of the Seas (below).

At each port of call, most cruise lines offer a good selection of shore excursions.

Above – An 18-hole championship course at Mullet Bay Resort, St Maarten.

Opposite – An Alaska floatplane takes passengers on a flightseeing trip to nearby mountains, glaciers and fjords.

Below – Passengers enjoy a few hours of snorkeling at Grand Cayman.

Sir Winston Churchill, consists of mountain peaks, deep green valleys and cliff-lined shores, tempered by a delightful climate.

Cruises to these island groups often include stops at the African mainland to visit the Moroccan ports of Tangier, Agadir (the 'Miami of Morocco') and Casablanca, with its beguiling blend of Arab bazaars and stately boulevards from the days of French colonialism.

River Cruises

Rivers were the lifeblood of past civilizations and today they offer cruise travelers a special type of holiday – a journey through history while enjoying the scenic beauty of these magnificent, meandering waterways. In sleek shallow-draft river vessels equipped with expansive viewing lounges, restaurants and comfortable cabins, passengers can travel the great rivers of America and Europe, and stop at famous cities and towns.

Choices of river cruises in North America include those on board the popular Mississippi riverboats, their steam engines driving both a huge paddlewheel on the stern and a pipe organ on deck. These river cruises are a trip back in time as passengers gaze at the passing sights of Mark Twain's beloved Mississippi while listening to Dixieland jazz and sipping mint juleps. The Delta Queen Steamboat Co. provides the most extensive cruises of the Mississippi and a river voyage can take in a number of its tributaries. Other small cruise ships journey along some of the great Pacific Coast rivers such as the Columbia, flowing along the border of Washington and Oregon, and the Sacramento, which wends deep into California's famous Napa Valley wine region.

The Rhine, principal river of Europe, rises in the Swiss Alps and flows through Switzerland, Liechtenstein, Austria, Germany, France and the Netherlands before emptying into the North Sea. A river cruise along this historic trade route takes passengers through breathtaking gorges, and past terraced vineyards and medieval castles perched atop historically strategic banks. The Romans first established forts and colonies along the Rhine's western banks, followed by robber barons of the Middle Ages who built castles along this important trade artery and exacted heavy tolls from passing ships and barges.

The Danube, less busy than the Rhine, rises from two sources in Germany's Black Forest and flows into Austria, past Linz and Vienna, then skirts Hungary before turning to flow across its central region to Budapest. A whole day is usually spent in Vienna, which for centuries was one of the great cities of Europe and today is a fascinating place for visitors interested in art, music, architecture and those delicious pastries served at Viennese coffee houses.

The ancient empire of the Nile can also be explored on a river cruise.

The Nile – 'long river between the deserts' – is the heart of one of mankind's earliest civilizations. History here is measured not in centuries but in millennia. The Age of the Great Pyramids was from 2680-2565 BC and the ones located near modern-day Cairo are the largest and finest of their kind. Other monumental forms of architecture include great temples, their massive facades flanked by sloping towers and their entrances approached between rows of sculptured sphinxes.

WHAT LENGTH OF CRUISE?

Once you have decided where you would like to go on a cruise, the next step is deciding what length of cruise you would like to take. For the first-time cruiser, a short three- to seven-day cruise is perhaps the best choice. This gives a person a taste of what cruising is like without committing a great deal of time and money to a new type of vacation. Also, because cruise fares are generally calculated on a per diem (daily) basis, you won't be paying a premium for taking a short versus a long cruise .

Short cruises have been riding a crest of popularity and are the fastest-growing segment of the industry. As a result, cruise lines, which used to assign older ships for mini-cruises, are now dedicating new ships to this type of cruise. Those departing from Miami for the Bahamas are especially popular, and people planning a Florida vacation can easily include a quick cruise in their holiday plans.

Vacationers traveling to other parts of North America will find a cruise opportunity is never far away. Throughout the summer and fall, New York is the base port for seven-day cruises to Bermuda, and Montreal is the base port for round-trip cruises of the St. Lawrence and Canada's Atlantic seaboard. Visitors to western Canada can combine a tour of the Canadian Rockies with a round-trip cruise out of Vancouver to Alaska. Seattle, San Francisco, Los Angeles, San Diego, Galveston and New Orleans all serve as home ports to cruise ships.

Of course some people may decide that, first cruise or not, they would rather opt for a longer itinerary. As long as you have chosen a ship that suits your tastes, you will not regret this decision. In fact, people who take a seven-day cruise often say afterwards they didn't want to get off the ship at the end of the trip. By then they had become familiar with the ship and, having quite naturally fallen into a rhythm of shipboard life, could quite happily have continued the cruise for another week or so.

Pick the number of days you would like to spend on a cruise and there will likely be an itinerary to suit your plans. Whether you opt for a seven-day cruise of the Western Caribbean or a 100-day round-the-world cruise, there is an excellent selection in cruise lengths for most parts of the world.

A vacation on board a cruise ship can be spent however each passenger pleases, such as lounging at poolside.

WHICH SHIP

Although every ship has its own personality, it's helpful to know the general category to which it belongs. The following section explains the different ship categories and some of the criteria you should consider when deciding which cruise vessel best suits your personality and travel budget.

TYPES OF SHIPS:
Classic Liners

The revival of shipboard travel, which began in the late 1960s, came in time to save some real beauties of the great transatlantic era which remain quite different from modern cruise ships. Designed for the rigors of an ocean crossing, the classic liners were long and sleek with heavy riveted plating, deep keels and sheltered deck space to shield passengers from inclement weather. The cabins tend to be roomy with plenty of closet space, especially those in the former first-class sections of the ship, but the corridors are generally narrower than in modern ships. Public areas create an atmosphere of tradition and refinement, with such features as grand staircases and original wood paneling, brass fixtures and stained glass. Public rooms in those days were actually set aside for smoking and featured leather-lined walls to absorb the smoke.

The attractions of these ships are varied and somewhat ambiguous. Some passengers like the look of older ships – many of which are maintained exactly as they were first built and command a loyal following. A number of classic ships have undergone dramatic changes to their interiors, thus bringing the best of both worlds to cruise passengers who like the appearance of a classic ship but want modern conveniences. Older, steam-driven ships are generally smoother than contemporary ships, which use diesel engines, and they ride a bad sea better with their fine bows and narrower stern sections.

The *QE2* was, in 1969, the last of the classic liners to be launched. Other classic liners still in service are the *Canberra* (launched in 1961), the *Norway* (launched as the *France* in 1962), the *Meridian* (launched as the *Galileo* in 1963), and the *Rotterdam* (launched in 1959).

P&O's *Canberra*, an enduring favorite with British cruisers, was refurbished in 1992 and sails the Mediterranean, Iberia, the Caribbean and around the world. Norwegian Cruise Line's *Norway*, which underwent a multi-million-dollar conversion in 1979/80, is dedicated to Caribbean waters year round. The *Meridian*, owned by Celebrity Cruises, was virtually rebuilt in 1990, with over $70 million invested to give this classic a thoroughly modern interior for her Bermuda and Caribbean cruise clientele. The *Rotterdam*, Holland America's flagship, embarks on Alaska cruises each summer and on a variety of itineraries the rest of the year. Cunard's *QE2*, extensively refurbished in 1987 and again in late 1994, provides regular transatlantic crossings as well as cruise holidays to other parts of the world.

It's hard to say how much longer these classic liners will remain in service, but for now they offer cruises reminiscent of a bygone era.

Modern Cruise Liners

The early 1980s marked a turning point in the cruise industry. As more and more people discovered the merits of a cruise holiday, the demand for additional ships began to surge. This new breed of ship was designed not for long ocean voyages but for coastal cruising and island hopping. In between ports of call, passengers of the '80s wanted – and got – plenty of diversions. Thus the new ships were dubbed 'floating resorts' because of their large outdoor decks, swimming pools, show lounges and casinos. Cabins were fitted with picture windows instead of portholes, some even with sliding glass doors that opened onto private verandas.

Traditionalists decried the boxy look of these new ships, as well as the fact that cabins were generally smaller than on classic liners. The rationale behind smaller cabin space was that passengers now spent far more time in the public areas and at the various ports of call than they did in their cabins. The new liners were designed as one-class ships, with every passenger enjoying access to all of the ship's lavish public areas.

Some trademark ships of the 1980s are Royal Caribbean Cruise Line's *Song of America*, Princess Cruises' *Royal Princess* and Holland America's *Nieuw Amsterdam* and *Noordam* (sister ships). They remain outstanding ships, for they offer many passengers a satisfying balance of facilities and size.

Megaships

While the new ships of the '80s were built to accommodate from 500 to 1,500 passengers, the megaships of the '90s are being designed to carry between 1,500 and 2,500 passengers. Their superstructures are similar to the '80s cruise liner, but they are built on a larger scale. Towering a dozen or more stories high and topped with expansive sun and sports decks, these megaships are more than floating resorts – they are floating holiday communities.

Royal Caribbean Cruise Line's new *Legend of the Seas* has a golf course on its upper deck and Princess Cruises' new *Sun Princess* is 14 stories high, contains five swimming pools, and requires a full-time gardener to tend the ship's lushly landscaped interior. Carnival Cruise Lines' new *Carnival Destiny* will be the first cruise ship to exceed 100,000 gross registered tons when it enters service in late 1996 and its features include four swimming pools, one with a three deck high water slide. This ship, the largest ever built, is too big to transit Panama Canal.

Luxury Small Ships

In contrast to the megaships are the intimate luxury ships carrying 100 to 300 passengers. Being aboard one of these upscale vessels is similar to being on board a billionaire's private yacht. The service is attentive and personalized, and the ships can pull into smaller ports than can their larger cousins. The on-board facilities are not as extensive as on the large liners, but all appointments are of the highest quality and some of the features are unique, such as a stern that folds out into a swimming platform from which passengers can partake in various water sports while the ship is at anchor. *Seabourn Spirit*, *Seabourn Pride*, and Cunard's *Sea Goddess I* and *II* are examples of luxury small ships.

Expedition Ships

Also comparatively small in size, carrying 100 to 200 passengers, expedition ships have a casual atmosphere with an emphasis on learning about the areas being explored. Guest lecturers, slideshows and well-stocked reference libraries are standard features. With their shallow drafts, these vessels can pull into small ports and remote anchorages where passengers are taxied ashore in rubber landing craft. The chance to observe wildlife in a pristine setting is a major appeal of these types of cruise vessels, which are popular in Alaska and other wilderness areas.

Sailing Vessels (Tall Ships)

The romance of sail is captured in sail-powered cruise vessels ranging from small windjammers to large clipper-style ships that carry a few hundred passengers. While all have an engine on board to help propel the vessel under certain conditions, the sails are raised much of the time and passengers are often encouraged to get involved in their handling through informal sailing classes. Life on board these vessels is unstructured and, when at anchor, passenger activities usually include beach picnics and watersports. Cabins are often modest and meals less elaborate than on cruise liners, although some sailing vessels, such as the Windstar fleet, offer luxury accommodations and service. Sail-powered cruise vessels are popular in the Caribbean and South Pacific.

River Cruise Vessels

Carrying up to 100 passengers, these long sleek vessels are custom-designed for river cruising. Facilities may include a small health club and theater, but more often consist of an upper-deck swimming pool, whirlpool, and canopied deck chair area for those who prefer sitting in the shade as their vessel glides past scenic shores. An enclosed viewing lounge with large windows provides a comfortable vantage for observing the passing sights, with historical background provided by onboard lecturers who are experts in their academic fields.

The vessel remains docked overnight, traveling only during daylight hours. The itinerary is what's important to a passenger booking a river cruise, so the emphasis is less on facilities and activities than on a refined holiday for those who appreciate and want to learn more about the history and culture of the area being cruised.

DETERMINING A SHIP'S ATMOSPHERE

They say a 'happy ship' is one with a happy crew. It might be added that this maxim also applies to the passengers. And no passenger is happy unless he or she feels comfortable with a ship's atmosphere. A number of factors determine each ship's prevailing atmosphere, including the ship's

Group activities include joining a scheduled tour of the ship's bridge where junior officers explain the basics of navigation to interested passengers.

size, the level of accommodation and service, and the age group it attracts.

A ship's interior space is measured in gross registered tons and the higher the tonnage, the larger the ship in terms of total on-board space. The new megaships are not necessarily longer or wider than their predecessors but they have a taller superstructure (i.e. more decks) which is reflected in size measurements of over 70,000 tons.

Ships are often 'rated' (given 1 to 5 stars) on a wide range of criteria, including design, appearance, cleanliness, decor, cuisine, service and entertainment. Two objective yardsticks that are somewhat useful in determining a ship's level of comfort and service are the space ratio and the crew-to-passenger ratio. The first measurement will help you determine the amount of breathing room each passenger has on board. For instance, a ratio of 40+ is the ultimate in spaciousness, 20-30 is moderately spacious, and 10 is high density. The ratio of crew to passengers will determine the level of service. On luxury vessels there are almost as many crewmembers as passengers while ships in the mid-range price category generally have a ratio of one crewmember for every two to three passengers.

A cruise line's brochure will also hold clues to the type of vessel you are considering. Some emphasize their ships' luxury service while others focus more on the wide range of activities and high level of fun enjoyed by their passengers. Some lines attract a young crowd, others a mature clientele. One ship might be perfect for honeymooners while another is more suitable for families; one ship might appeal to a mature couple seeking quiet refinement and another will be attractive to passengers who like a casual atmosphere and sports-oriented activities.

A ship's character is also determined by the nationality of its officers. The naval academies of seafaring nations, such as Britain, Greece, Italy, and Norway, produce many of the officers who are employed by the cruise lines. Princess, for example, has British, Norwegian and Italian officers, while those running the ships of Carnival are Italian. Celebrity's officers are Greek, Holland America's are Dutch, and the officers of Royal Caribbean Cruise Line and Norwegian Cruise Line are usually from Norway.

The nationality of the service staff is another factor to consider. Senior service personnel are often of the same nationality as the officers, while those heading various subordinate departments might be from other countries. Many ships have an international staff, so your cabin steward, dining room waiter and bar staff could all be from different countries.

Last but not least is the prevailing nationality of the passengers. The majority of the world's cruise passengers are American, so the majority of cruise lines cater to English-speaking passengers. It is rare indeed to have problems with language aboard any ships departing from North America – all crew will have at least a basic knowledge of English.

The atmosphere and nationality of each cruise line is described in more detail in Chapter 5.

Honeymoons and Wedding Anniversaries

Newlyweds and couples seeking a romantic way to celebrate a special wedding anniversary often choose a cruise. To add to the allure of such a holiday, most cruise lines provide a few extras for these special couples. On the better cruise lines the perks almost always include a Captain's cocktail party for all newlyweds as well as a special cake and bottle of bubbly. Some cruise lines, for a very modest fee, will really lay on the goodies for honeymooners – cabin upgrades, champagne, bathrobes and flowers. If you are celebrating a wedding or an anniversary, be sure to tell your travel agent. You could be looking forward to some pleasant surprises during your cruise.

Theme and Special Interest Cruises

Theme cruises continue to grow in popularity as people increasingly want to get more out of their holiday than simply lying about on a beach. Many people are finding that they enjoy combining a special interest or hobby with a cruise vacation. Relaxed and free of any daily decision making, they can immerse themselves in pastimes they find stimulating and enjoyable. At the end of the cruise, they return home feeling recharged, savoring a sense of accomplishment for having improved, for instance, their golf swing or their appreciation of classical music.

Guest lecturers (often celebrity authors) are becoming quite common on cruises around the world. Cruise lines will sometimes present a number of speakers on one theme, such as photography or financial planning, or host a floating musical celebration, examples being big band cruises (with dancing under the stars) and jazz festivals at sea. Everything from bridge tournaments to basketball coaching is offered, and these special cruises are growing in popularity and choices of theme. If you have an interest you would like to pursue with like-minded passengers, ask your cruise agent to check what's available for there's a good chance such a specialized cruise exists.

Expedition and river cruising are theme cruises of themselves, each cruise's theme determined by the region being visited. For instance, an expedition cruise of Alaska will focus on the glaciers, wildlife and native culture. A river cruise of the Nile will enlighten its passengers with an archaeological look at Ancient Egypt.

LAND TOURS

Passengers who fly to distant destinations to join a cruise are often tempted to include some land travel in the trip. Cruise companies have anticipated this and they offer passengers a wide range of pre- and post-cruise land tours.

Caribbean cruises, many of which use Miami and Fort Lauderdale as their base ports, present a perfect opportunity for passengers to see the sights of Florida before or after their cruise. Orlando's Walt Disney World, Epcot Center, Everglades National Park, and the Florida Keys are all major holiday destinations, as are the beach resorts that line much of the state's coastline.

Mediterranean cruisers can opt for a rail trip to England on board the Venice-to-London Orient Express. And the Canadian Rockies and Denali National Park are popular destinations for cruise passengers looking to extend their Alaskan cruise with a land tour.

An African land adventure might include a few nights in Cape Town followed by visits to the Cape of Good Hope, wineries, ostrich farms and cheetah ranches. Highlights of an extended Australian cruise include such contrasting settings as the cosmopolitan city of Sydney and the outback town of Alice Springs; the stark sight of Ayers Rock and the thriving submarine life of the Great Barrier Reef.

Passengers cruising the Far East invariably choose to include a visit to Beijing where the Forbidden City, Summer Palace, and nearby Great Wall await those fascinated by this ancient empire. Japan is another cruise destination that lures passengers inland to view its imperial palaces, Buddhist temples and meditative gardens.

Whatever part of the world you visit by cruise ship, you can usually extend your stay through land tour packages organized by the cruise line with transportation often a combination of coach, rail and jet travel.

SHIPBOARD ACTIVITIES

The one word cruise lines fear above all else is boredom. Even the most humble of ships will make a decent effort to keep its passengers amused, and a number of sports and recreational opportunities are offered by the ship's cruise director on a daily basis. Not every ship offers all the activities we've listed here, but most will offer at least some and it's possible to find out, before booking, which ships offer the activities you consider essential to an enjoyable cruise vacation.

Walking, for example, is popular with everyone, which is why almost all ships have what is called a promenade deck – named from the days when promenade meant a stroll. Now this term means anything from a fast walk to a slow jog but its common purpose remains exercising in the fresh air. Ships with a teak promenade deck are especially delightful to walk on and most promenade decks encircle the entire ship.

Probably the next most common exercise facility is some sort of gym room, where those who enjoy a more concentrated regime of activity will be able to work out on equipment or to the directions of a fitness instructor. A swimming pool is another standard feature on modern cruise ships, but from here on the range of activities is quite varied. The size and class of ship will, to some extent, determine the recreational possibilities.

The Following List Is A Sampling of Shipboard Activities

Athletics:
Walk a Mile on the
    Promenade Deck
Low-Impact Aerobics /
    High-Impact Aerobics
Lower Back and Abdominal
    Exercises
Golf Chipping
Mens and Ladies Golf
    Putting Tournaments
Dance Classes
Deck Tennis, Football and
    Cricket
Volleyball, Basketball and
    Table Tennis Tournaments
Quoits Tournaments

Health & Beauty:
Fashion Shows
Hair, Beauty and Fitness
    Demonstrations
Skin Care and Cosmetic
    Demonstrations
Slimming, Toning and
    Nutrition Talks

Games:
Backgammon Tournaments
Gin Rummy Games
Duplicate Bridge
    Championships
Blackjack Tournaments

Games, Con't
International Horseracing
Quizzes and Panel Games
Jackpot Bingo
Dominoes, Scrabble and
    Monopoly
Chess and Checkers

Ship Tours *(guided tours of various working areas of the ship which are conducted by junior officers and members of the ship's staff):*
Kitchen
Navigation Bridge
Engine Room
Back Stage
Casino
Artwork & Antiques

Classes & Demonstrations:
Cooking Classes with an
    Executive Chef
Cheese Fondue
    Demonstrations
Vegetable Carving and Ice
    Carving Demonstrations
Art of Napkin Folding and
    Flower Arranging
Photography Tips from the
    Ship's Chief
    Photographer
Learn to play Blackjack,
    Craps and Roulette

CHAPTER THREE

DID YOU KNOW?

Some Interesting Facts About Cruising

Cruising is Not Prohibitively Expensive

Cruising used to be very expensive, but no longer. In real terms, the cost of cruising has been steadily decreasing and it is now one of the most economical vacations available when all daily costs are taken into account. Your accommodation, meals and entertainment are all included in the price of your cruise ticket. Even your airfare – if you have to fly to the port of embarkation – is available at an air/sea package rate. When you leave home at the beginning of your cruise vacation, you already know exactly what the entire trip will cost.

Of course you will probably incur some extra expenses, but these are entirely at your discretion. Organized shore excursions, for example, will cost extra, as will personal services such as haircuts and massages on board the ship. Alcoholic drinks ordered in lounges and dining rooms will also be charged to your cabin, as will purchases at the on-board shops. However, a person could theoretically step on board a cruise ship and not spend another penny for the duration of the trip.

How, you might ask, has cruising become so economical? The answer – economy of scale and competitiveness. Many of the cruise companies have built large ships that carry high numbers of passengers, and this increased capacity has allowed them to reduce costs. While some luxury ships still serve an upscale clientele, the average vacationer can now board a cruise ship and enjoy its relaxed ambiance and wide array of facilities for a fraction of what a similar cruise would have cost 20 years ago. As more and more people take to cruising – as did more than 5 1/2 million travelers last year – new ships are being added to the current selection. This allows customers to shop around for the cruise best suited to their budget and personal taste. It's a competitive market for the cruise lines and a shopper's paradise for the cruise customer.

Cruises Fit Into Any Vacation Schedule

Cruising used to appeal mainly to people with lots of leisure time on their hands. Not so today. With jet planes whisking passengers to their ports of embarkation, cruises are now offered in lengths ranging from three days to round-the-world voyages of three months.

Cruises of three to four days duration are a good way for first-time cruisers to test the waters and see if cruising appeals to them. Highly popular are the one- to two-week cruises, which fit into most people's vacation schedules. With time at a premium as people juggle their work commitments and personal lives, a one- to two-week cruise is an ideal way to visit a number of destinations in a short period of time, yet still feel relaxed and refreshed at the end of the holiday.

The major cruise lines provide an array of supervised activities for their young passengers.

Cruising is for All Age Groups

The average age of cruise passengers is steadily dropping, with almost 40 per cent of new passengers now under the age of 35. Cruising has become a novelty for people who grew up with jet travel and fast-paced lifestyles. They enjoy the relaxed atmosphere of a ship and the freedom to do whatever they choose while on board.

Those who grew up in the Swinging '60s are now leading younger generations across the gangway onto ships where casualness has replaced conformity and fun takes precedence over etiquette. Not that common courtesy has been tossed overboard, but good manners are now practiced with a friendly openness.

Young singles, newlyweds, couples with children, empty nesters and retired people all enjoy cruising for different reasons. A cruise holiday can be whatever you want it to be – from slow paced to action packed – which is why passengers of all ages enjoy shipboard travel. Children are often the biggest fans of cruising. They are free of the shadow of their parents who don't feel the need to check on their youngsters wherever they go. In addition to having fun at the various activities organized for them, children enjoy the special treatment they receive from the cruise staff, who often dote on their younger passengers. Many children thrive in the attention they receive.

Family reunions and cruises make a perfect combination, especially for grandparents whose children and grandchildren are spread about the country. A cruise is an ideal opportunity for an extended family to spend some relaxing time together without the distraction of meal preparation and housekeeping. During school vacations, most cruise lines provide extra youth counsellors and organized children's activities. Christmastime is especially suited to family reunions with ships decked out in festive greenery and the holiday season celebrated with carolers, traditional fare and even a visit from Santa.

Cruising is Not Restrictive

A common concern among people contemplating their first cruise is that the ship will seem too small and claustrophobic. They don't realize how different a cruise ship is from a hotel. Entire decks of large cruise ships are devoted to public areas that include restaurants, lounges, shops, swimming pools and recreation areas. A person could actually get lost on some of the larger ships, and locator maps are placed near stairwells and elevators to help passengers navigate their way around the ship. Many passengers find it takes a good week on board the ship before they have explored all of its public space and can find their way around the entire ship with ease.

There is No Forced Sociability on Board

Many people who haven't yet cruised envisage a typical cruise as having no end of organized activities in which they must partake. Yes, there are plenty of group activities for those who enjoy meeting people, but there aren't non-stop announcements and cruise employees aren't continually herding reluctant passengers off to the next event. The daily program, slipped under your cabin door, is what keeps you informed of organized activities and you can ignore any or all of them if you so choose.

Passengers seeking quiet solitude can usually find just that. They can request a table for two in the dining room, rather than a larger table for six or eight people. They can slip into the library or find themselves a quiet viewing lounge or deck chair in which to read and chat quietly with a companion. The outside decks are often surprisingly empty of fellow passengers, depending on the time of day and the ship's location. And of course, passengers can always retire to the privacy of their cabin whenever they like.

The operative word is 'control'. You have complete control of how you spend your time on a cruise vacation.

A Trunk of New Clothes Isn't Necessary to go Cruising

Go ahead and buy some new clothes if you like – that's part of the fun of taking a vacation – but your wardrobe probably contains everything you need for cruising.

For daytime activities on the ship and in port, casual and comfortable clothes are the norm. You'll want to pack something a bit dressier for semi-formal nights in the dining room, such as a skirt or dress for the ladies and a sports jacket for the men. For the one or two formal evenings on the ship, you will need nothing more special than a cocktail dress for the ladies, and a jacket and tie for the men. You can, if you like, pack a sequined evening gown or tuxedo, but this is not mandatory.

Passengers are usually asked to wear a cover-up over their bathing suits before entering the dining room for lunch or when strolling through other indoor areas of the ship. And on casual evenings, jeans, shorts and t-shirts are considered a bit too casual in the dining room.

The ship's daily program will advise you of each evening's dress code, but this is fairly flexible. Most passengers do respect the dress code and many enjoy the opportunity to look their best at dinner each night. After all, part of the shipboard dining experience is the elegant atmosphere and attentive service, so why not dress the part?

Onboard activities range from fun to educational.
 Above – A golf chipping tournament at the lido pool.
Opposite – A ship's naturalist explains the dynamics of a tidewater glacier.
Below – Wine tasting is enjoyed on board a culinary cruise.

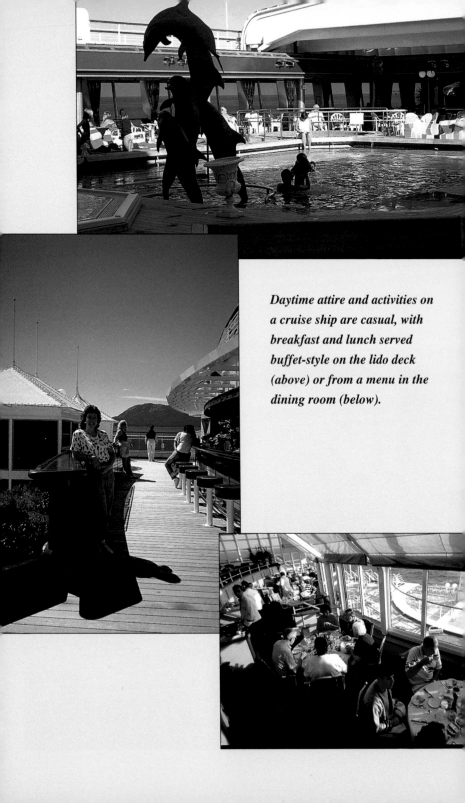

Daytime attire and activities on a cruise ship are casual, with breakfast and lunch served buffet-style on the lido deck (above) or from a menu in the dining room (below).

The public lounges, often quiet during the day, come to life each evening with music to dance by and, in the main show lounge, lavish stage productions.

A cruise ship acts as a shoreside hotel while in port, from which its guests can set off independently to explore the local sights (opposite) or join an organized excursion to nearby archaeological and cultural sites (below).

Fine Dining is Still Part of the Cruise Experience

One thing that hasn't changed on board cruise ships is the exceptional cuisine. Most people embark on a cruise anticipating lavish meals and they are rarely disappointed. With a new lunch and dinner menu presented daily, from which you can order as many courses as you like, a cruise can be an epicurean delight. And there is enough variety in the menu to suit all tastes – from basic to gourmet.

The meals enjoyed in the course of a cruise could quickly add up to hundreds of dollars if a passenger were paying for them individually at comparable restaurants on shore. Yet, surprisingly, these high-quality and varied meals account for only a fraction of the price a cruise ticket. It's estimated that food generally accounts for about 10 per cent of a cruise line's total operating costs, which is less than the cost of fuel.

On a ship holding 1,200 passengers, there are over 5,000 meals prepared each day. A typical kitchen staff on a ship this size consists of the Executive Chef, 11 Chefs de Partie (Department Heads), 12 Aides de Cuisine, four Demi Chefs, 26 assistant cooks, 14 pantry personnel, and 26 workers in charge of cleaning the kitchen and processing the garbage. Provisions for a seven-day cruise might include 8,000 pounds of beef, 36 pounds of caviar, 680 pounds of cheese, 465 gallons of ice cream, 25,000 pounds of fresh vegetables, 24,000 pounds of fresh fruit, 7,000 bottles of beer, and 1,600 bottles of wine.

Everyone Cruises 'First Class'

On today's cruise ships, everyone cruises 'first class'. All shipboard facilities, be it the swimming pool, show lounge, cinema or gymnasium, are open to all passengers, regardless of the deck on which their cabin is located. On a few cruise liners the passengers are assigned to specific dining rooms according to their grade of cabin, but all other public areas are accessible to everyone. No one misses out on anything. There is always room in the show lounge for those who want to take in that evening's entertainment, and there's no lining up for drinks – these will be brought to your table. Everyone receives the same service and enjoys the same cruise experience regardless of the cabin they booked.

The size and location of cabin is more important to some passengers than to others. Some feel they spend such little time in their cabin, it's unnecessary to pay for something larger. Others enjoy retiring to a stateroom that is more spacious and comfortable than a standard cabin and these people are willing to pay more for their personal accommodation. However, regardless of what you eventually decide regarding choice of cabin, the rest of the ship is yours to fully enjoy.

Seasickness

When ocean liners regularly crossed the North Atlantic during the first half of this century, it was not unusual for passengers to get seasick – especially if the ship was pitching or rolling in the big seas of a winter storm. Today the majority of cruises take place in protected coastal waters and most passengers experience little, if any, discomfort on a regular one- to two-week cruise.

The aim of modern ship travel is no longer to get from one side of an ocean to the other, but to meander from port to port, so a ship's routes do not generally entail long stretches of open-water sailing. Cruise itineraries are planned to coincide with a region's fair-weather season and accurate forecasting allows a captain to alter his ship's course if bad weather is approaching.

Modern cruise ships also have stabilizers – fin-like appendages that can be extended from each side of the ship just below its waterline – that will prevent a ship from rolling excessively in a big sea.

Still, some people are susceptible to motion sickness but they needn't suffer in silence while cruising. There are a number of effective remedies at their disposal, including such simple solutions as standing out on deck in the fresh air, or nibbling on crackers and sipping ginger ale. Some people find that wearing special wristbands, the balls of which rest on an acupressure point, is all they need to prevent queasiness. Others obtain prescription medication from their doctor before leaving home. Those susceptible passengers who are caught unprepared can visit the ship's front office or infirmary to obtain tablets that reduce motion sickness.

Should a passenger become concerned about their condition, medical attention can be sought immediately with the ship's qualified medical personnel. However, motion sickness is rarely a serious problem on most cruises and those who experience it usually find it is short lived.

Trip of a Lifetime?

Many people delay taking a cruise until they have a special reason for doing so. For years they talk about 'one day taking a cruise' – possibly to celebrate a milestone wedding anniversary or a long-anticipated retirement. Yet, a cruise needn't be considered a once-in-a-lifetime experience.

With today's fly/cruise packages, shorter itineraries and cheaper fares, a cruise vacation can become an annual holiday for those who like to travel. Cruise lines and their booking agents value their repeat passengers, often offering them first choice on special packages and generous early-booking discounts. Seasoned passengers, rather than tiring of the cruise experience, usually find that they get more and more out of cruising with

Relaxation takes many forms on a cruise, including a casual game of shuffleboard.

each trip they go on. They come to know which cruise lines appeal to their personal tastes and which type of ship they prefer, and they may discover that for them one of the best ways to see the world is from the deck of a ship.

Repeat cruisers are usually well-traveled and enjoy all types of holidays, so they find that cruising meshes well with their other travel experiences. They might, for instance, go on a one-week cruise of the Caribbean, then return the next year to an island resort they briefly visited while in port. The following year they're off to the Mediterranean, cruising to four or five ports of call, with a view to possibly returning for a longer, land-based stay in one the countries they visited by ship. Cruising, for many, becomes another mode of travel and adds variety to their vacation choices.

CHAPTER FOUR

PORTS OF CALL

A Close Look At Worldwide Cruise Routes

This chapter is designed to give you a closer look at the cruising areas briefly described in Chapter 2, with highlights of some of the popular ports of call.

ALASKA

Each year Alaska attracts a record number of cruise passengers who come to see this vast and rugged coastline of mountains, forests, glaciers and fjords. From May to October, ships wend their way along the narrow, winding channels of the Inside Passage – so named because it lies within a long chain of coastal islands which act as a buffer from the open waters of the North Pacific. Wildlife sighted along the way can include whales, dolphins, porpoises, sea otters, bears and bald eagles.

The majority of cruise ships trace two popular routes. The Inside Passage route is a round-trip, one-week cruise from Vancouver, Canada; the Glacier Route is a seven-day, line voyage between Vancouver and Anchorage that includes the Inside Passage, Gulf of Alaska and Prince William Sound. An Inside Passage cruise usually includes a close look at some tidewater glaciers, such as those at the head of narrow, cliff-sided Tracy Arm, or those found in the many inlets of Glacier Bay – a body of water that was completely filled with ice as recently as 200 years ago when Britain's George Vancouver sailed past its ice-clogged entrance.

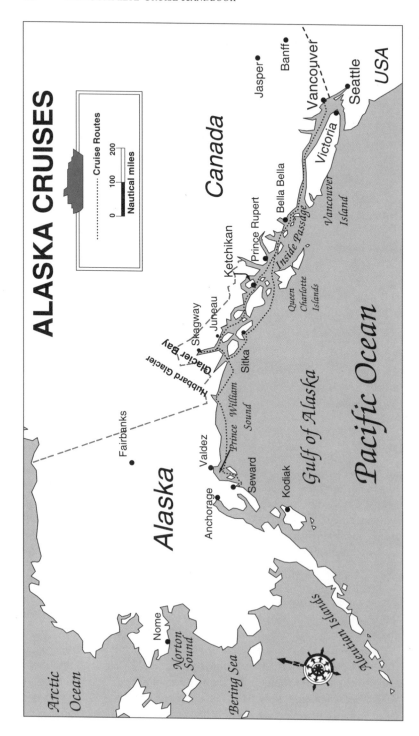

Major Ports of the Inside Passage

Ports of call along the Inside Passage are situated on the edge of islands or at the base of coastal mountains, and most are accessible only by water or air. Wedged between mountains and sea, Alaskan ports have scenic settings and friendly atmospheres. Their pioneer heritage is evidenced in wooden warehouses, canneries and boardwalks built on pilings. Native totem poles are on display at various locations. The moist maritime climate of coastal Alaska has produced dense forests of towering evergreens that surround these pockets of habitation. The ports are compact and can easily be explored on foot. Many visitors, while their ship is in port, take excursions to the outlying wilderness areas to view glaciers and wildlife.

Ketchikan, a cannery town founded in the late 1800s, is situated at the mouth of Ketchikan Creek where salmon can be seen swimming upstream as they return to their spawning grounds. The region's vibrant native culture is reflected in numerous totem pole displays. A popular wilderness excursion is the float plane trip over the beautiful Misty Fjords, with stunning views of alpine lakes and steep-sided channels that were carved by retreating glaciers.

Juneau is named after one of the prospectors who discovered gold here in 1880, and this scenic state capital contains local sights ranging from the Red Dog Saloon to the Governor's Mansion. Juneau also offers visitors the opportunity to take a float plane or helicopter flight over the sprawling Juneau Icefield. Helicopters land on a glacier so that passengers, wearing special boots, can walk across its icy surface and peer down its deep crevasses. Also popular is the flight to nearby Taku Harbor for a salmon bake at a rustic lodge.

The boomtown of **Skagway** sprang into being in 1897 during the Klondike Gold Rush and its streets are lined with original falsefronted buildings that now house gift shops and visitor centers. A sleepy village during the winter months, Skagway bustles with visitors throughout the summer. The town is set at the head of beautiful Lynn Canal, bounded by snowcapped mountains. Arriving cruise passengers can ride the narrow gauge railway that retraces the route taken by thousands of gold prospectors as they climbed over the mountains to reach the Klondike.

The fishing port of **Sitka** is the former capital of Russian America and its attractions include St. Michael's Cathedral and cannon-ringed Castle Hill, where the offical transfer of Alaska to the United States took place in 1867.

The Glacier Route

Ships proceeding beyond the Inside Passage into the Gulf of Alaska often pull into Yakutat Bay, where massive Hubbard Glacier resides at the head of this mountain-ringed bay. **Prince William Sound**, situated at the top of the Gulf of Alaska, contains Alaska's highest concentration of tidewater glaciers and is the highlight of a glacier cruise. Its mainland shores are surrounded by snowy peaks and indented by dozens of glacier-carved fjords.

A northbound glacier cruise usually terminates in the fishing port of **Seward**, on the Kenai Peninsula, where passengers board coaches for a scenic three-hour drive to Anchorage, where they connect with land tours or a flight home. A city surrounded by wilderness, **Anchorage** is an interesting blend of modern metropolis and Alaskan bush town. On clear days, Mount McKinley – North America's highest peak – can be seen from downtown Anchorage.

ATLANTIC ISLES

The **Azores**, resort islands of beaches and vineyards, were reached by Portugese sailors in the early 1400s and were once the site of naval battles between England and Spain. Today this farflung outpost of Portugal is the site of NATO air bases. Ponta Delgada is a popular port of call.

The verdant, mountainous **Madeira Islands**, lying 350 miles off Morocco, were originally known to the Romans as the Purple Islands. Rediscovered by the Portuguese in the early 1400s, settlement took place under orders of Prince Henry the Navigator. The British temporarily occupied the islands in the early 19th century, but today they are an autonomous region of Portugal. Their steep slopes are covered with patchwork fields of green and dotted with villages of red-roofed houses. Flowers such as bougainvillea and hibiscus flourish here and one of the world's highest sea cliffs – Cabo Girao – provides a spectacular ocean view. The port of Funchal was a favorite winter retreat of Sir Winston Churchill, who came here on painting holidays. Situated on a beautiful harbor at the base of a mountain, Funchal has a bustling local market where fresh flowers, hand-sewn linens and wickerwork are sold. Fine local wines can be enjoyed at one of the bodegas and afternoon tea is served at the classic Reids Hotel.

Spain's **Canary Islands**, volcanic in origin, have a recorded history dating back to 40 BC. An important base for voyages to the Americas, they were frequently raided by pirates and privateers such as Sir Francis Drake. The islands visited by cruise ships are Gran Canaria, Tenerife and Lanzarote with its black and red beaches, bubbling geysers and grottoes containing emerald-colored water. Las Palmas, only 67 miles from the African coast, is the capital of Gran Canaria. Cruise passengers can visit the house in which Columbus once stayed or head to the sand dunes and beaches at nearby Maspalomas. At Tenerife the ships dock in Santa Cruz where duty free shops await visitors. To the south are resorts and beaches of soft volcanic sand. The snowcovered summit of Mount Teide – Spain's highest point – dominates the island, its valleys filled with banana and pineapple plantations.

Morocco, on the northwest coast of Africa, is often included in cruises to the Atlantic Isles. One of its popular ports is Casablanca, well known to fans of the classic Hollywood film of the same name starring Humphrey Bogart and Ingrid Bergman. Casablanca was also where the Allied leaders met in 1943. From Casablanca visitors can embark on excursions to Marrakech, an ancient red-walled Royal City of narrow alleyways, sultan's gardens, palaces, and an atmosphere evocative of the Arabian nights. Tangier is another fascinating Moroccon port situated at the crossroads of Europe and Africa. Visitors can stroll the winding, hilly streets, each one featuring a different group of artisans where you can barter for handcrafted goods. Other attractions are a Sultan's garden and the palace of Dar el Makhzen. Nearby Kasbah features a palace protected by fortress walls.

BERMUDA

The number of cruise ships allowed to visit Bermuda is closely monitored to prevent overcrowding of these beautiful islands. A handful of cruise lines offer regular sailings out of New York from May through October. With 55,000 people living in an area of of 21 square miles, Bermudians have also taken measures to prevent traffic congestion and air pollution by allowing only one car per family. Visitors can tour the interconnecting chain of islands on rented mopeds, in hired taxis, or on the local blue-and-pink buses.

There are three cruise ship ports in Bermuda – King's Wharf at West End, Hamilton Harbour and St. George – and most ships visit two of them, although some will remain at one port. Distances between ports are not great and, during a typical four-day stay, it's easy to see the entire island chain regardless of where your ship docks and becomes a floating hotel. Many people head to the south coast where beautiful beaches range from long stretches of pink sand to tiny, protected coves. Diving and snorkeling are excellent in the clear waters of these reef-ringed islands. Only two miles across at its widest point, Bermuda has over a hundred beaches and eight golf courses. Other natural attractions include caves, grottoes and sea arches.

Bermuda is a British dependency and was discovered by Virginia-bound British colonists in 1609 when they shipwrecked on these islands. Their maritime and colonial history can be seen when strolling King's Square in St. George or visiting Gibb's Hill Lighthouse and the local museums. Avid shoppers can let loose in Hamilton, the commercial center of Bermuda, where shop-lined Front Street overlooks the harbor.

CARIBBEAN

Cruise ships began visiting the Caribbean in the 1960s when jet planes became the new mode of trans-Atlantic travel and shipping companies sought new roles for their gracious ocean liners. Today the Caribbean is the most popular cruising area in the world, and for good reason. The allure of this island-dotted turquoise sea is legendary, but natural beauty is not its only attribute. Each of the Caribbean's diverse island nations has its own history and ecosystem, which have helped shape its inhabitants and their societies.

The British, French, Dutch and Danish all explored these islands in the wake of Spanish expeditions first led by Christopher Columbus. Spain initially established forts along the Caribbean mainland and on most the Greater Antilles – the larger islands of the West Indies. Other European nations scooped up the smaller islands – the Lesser Antilles – left unclaimed by Spain. Meanwhile, the native inhabitants were all but obliterated by European colonialism, with a pocket of surviving Carib natives now living on Dominica. Africans were brought to these islands as slaves to work on the sugar plantations and they remain the dominant racial group of the Caribbean, setting the tone with their love of rhythmic music and bold colors.

Some of the islands are volcanic in origin, with mountainous terrains, while others are low coral islands. Most are ringed with beautiful beaches bordered by palm trees and tropical flowers. Caribbean in origin, and often seen slung between two palm trees, is the hammock - which aptly sums up the relaxed pace and mood of these sun-blessed islands.

There are many cruise lines in the Caribbean offering different itineraries along three fairly defined routes which are commonly referred to as Western, Eastern and Southern Caribbean cruises. Western Caribbean cruises often include stops at Jamaica, Grand Caymen, Cozumel and the Mexican mainland. Eastern cruises take in the Bahamas, St Thomas (one of the US Virgin Islands) and other islands of the Lesser Antilles, a popular one being St Maarten. A Southern cruise takes in the rest of the Lesser Antilles, destinations such as Barbados, Grenada and Curacao. Caribbean cruises depart from various base ports and range in length from three days to two weeks.

Base Ports

San Juan on the island of Puerto Rico was founded in 1508 by Ponce de Leon. A major Spanish port, it contains El Morro – the most extensive fortress in the Caribbean. Today this city of narrow cobbled streets and sunny plazas is the capital of Puerto Rico and a base port for cruises of the Eastern and Southern Caribbean. A local museum is devoted to Pablo Casals, the Spanish virtuoso cellist and conductor who settled here.

The major base ports for the Caribbean are located in Florida and include **Fort Lauderdale**, a popular retirement community and tourist destination with its miles of soft sand beaches and canal-lined residential streets where yachts rather than cars are parked out front. **Miami** is the busiest port, especially for cruises to the Bahamas where turquoise-green water, white beaches, the British colonial architecture of Nassau, and the beach resorts on Paradise Island draw plenty of visitors.

Port Canaveral, with its proximity to the Kennedy Space Center and Walt Disney World, is also used by cruise ships, as is **Tampa** – ideally located for some pre- or post-cruise touring of Florida's Gulf Coast.

New Orleans, Louisiana, is another base port for Caribbean cruises. This fascinating city offers Creole culture, a French quarter, and numerous parks, gardens and world-famous restaurants.

Western Caribbean Ports

Cozumel is Mexico's only Caribbean island and the snorkeling here is superb in the extremely clear waters. Playa del Carmen and Cancun, located across the channel on the Yucatan Peninsula, are service ports for cruise passengers embarking on shore excursions to the area's Mayan ruins. These ancient sites include the walled city of Tulum, the pyramid-shaped temples at Chichen Itza, and the extensive ruins at Coba.

The British island of **Grand Cayman** also has clear waters for diving and visitors can take submarine and glass-bottom boat rides over the island's extensive coral reefs. Georgetown is the port of call and an international banking center. Seven Mile Beach is another attraction of Grand Cayman.

Jamaica is an island famous for its beautiful and varied scenery - mountain ranges, sparkling rivers, cascading waterfalls, and plenty of pristine beaches. Ships visiting Jamaica often call at **Ocho Rios** where a popular excursion is walking up the tiered stream bed of spectacular Dunn's River Falls.

Key West, Florida, is included in some Western Caribbean itineraries. The most southern point of the US mainland, Key West is only 60 miles from Cuba. This pretty town of tree-lined streets has long attracted bohemians and artists. Ernest Hemingway's former residence is now a popular attraction as is Mel Fisher's Treasure Museum.

Eastern & Southern Caribbean Ports

Aruba, Bonaire and **Curacao** are the ABC's of the Dutch Antilles that lie off the coast of Venezuela. Aruba's port of call is Oranjestad, its Dutch heritage evident in gabled row houses painted with bright Caribbean colors. Aruba offers fine beaches and clear water for snorkeling and diving.

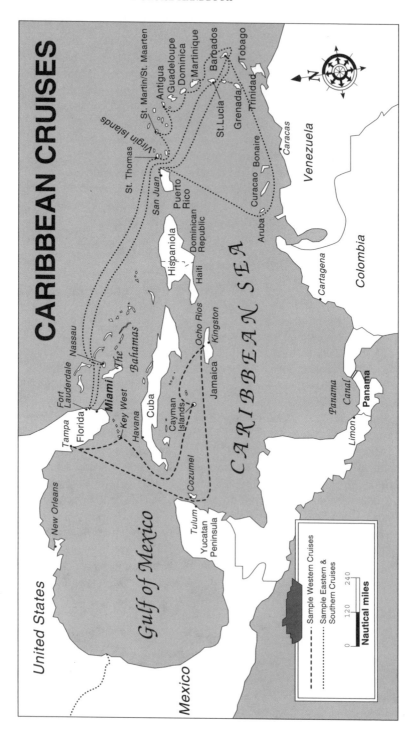

Bonaire's tiny harbour of Kralendijk is a pretty port with a bustling market place. Again, the island offers good snorkeling with its pastel corals and tropical fish. Huge flocks of pink flamingos live on the island.

Curacao's Willemstad is one of the prettiest Caribbean ports with its golden-colored gabled houses. Other historic architecture includes the Old Dutch Church (built in 1769) and one of the oldest synagogues in the Western Hemisphere, built in 1732. Curacao is well known for its orange-flavored liqueur of the same name.

Antigua, one of the Leeward Islands, has beautiful beaches and a British colonial history evidenced by Nelson's Dockyard at English Harbour.

Barbados is the most British of the Caribbean islands. Cricket is the national sport and the capital of Bridgetown has its own Trafalgar Square with Nelson's Column. The standard of living here is high and the scenery diverse. The island's west coast is lined with lovely swimming beaches; the rugged east coast, exposed to the Atlantic, is pounded by surf; and the interior is criss-crossed with narrow roads that lead through villages and past sugarcane plantations.

La Guaira is the port of access to **Caracas**, capital and largest city of Venezuela. Founded by the Spanish in 1567, the city is bordered by mountains to the north and hills to the south and, being more than 3,000 feet above sea level, has an ideal climate. Almost completely destroyed by an earthquake in 1812, Caracas is a modern city which experienced heavy immigration from Europe following World War II.

Cartagena, Columbia, was founded in 1533, its massive walls built to defend the port against marauding pirates. The view from its 17th century monastery is of Iberian palaces, shady plazas and narrow cobblestone streets where boutiques are housed in medieval dungeons.

Dominica, one of the least developed of the Caribbean islands, was named by Columbus who sailed by on a Sunday. The island's lush and mountainous terrain consists of untouched rainforest, hundreds of rivers and streams, and numerous waterfalls. Dominica offers some of the best wilderness hiking in the Caribbean.

On **Grenada**, the Spice Island, warm breezes carry the fragrance of cinnamon, nutmeg, cloves and vanilla. The capital of St George consists of a circular inner lagoon lined with pastel-painted warehouses and gabled buildings.

The tiny and unspoiled **Grenadines** contain private islands of pristine beaches and clear waters for snorkeling.

Guadeloupe consists of two distinctly different islands – one is mountainous and volcanic in origin and the other is a flat, coral-formed island ringed with white beaches. A French stronghold since 1635, its Creole culture mixes French, African and Indian influences.

Martinique was the birthplace of Napoleon's Josephine. Visited by Columbus in 1502, the island was colonized by the French in 1635. A mountainous island, its valleys are lush with sugar cane and pineapple plantations.

St Kitts was first colonized by the British in 1623 and the main port of Basseterre contains Government House and the Old Court House. It takes four hours for a leisurely drive around this entire island, with such stops along the way as Brimstone Hill Fort with views across the water to its Dutch sister island of St Eustatius.

St Lucia, fought over by the British and French, is a lush and mountainous island containing one of the Caribbean's most famous landmarks - the Pitons, which are twin conical peaks overlooking Soufriere Bay. Another beautiful spot on St Lucia is Marigot Bay which was used as a setting for the film Dr Doolittle.

The Dutch and the French decided to share the island of **St Maarten/St Martin.** Philipsburg is the Dutch port where good shopping bargains can be found. It's a short drive across the island to the French side and the pretty port of Marigot. Fine beaches, golf links, and sailing on board an America's Cup 12-metre yacht are some of the attractions for visitors to this popular island.

The busiest island in the Caribbean for cruise business is the US territory of **St Thomas**. Over 1,000 miles from Florida, this island has become

The St Thomas port of Charlotte Amalie, administrative center of the US Virgin Islands, is the Caribbean's busiest port with its duty-free shopping and beautiful beaches nearby.

known as a shopping mecca for all travelers to the Caribbean. The capital, Charlotte Amalie, has extensive dock facilities to accommodate the thousands of passengers who disembark here each year. A free port, the city was founded by Danes in the late 17th century and was the center of Danish colonial life. At one point during the first buccaneering phase of the Caribbean, the infamous Edward Teach – Blackbeard – made his home here and part of his castle remains as an inn and restaurant.

Today, Charlotte Amalie is the administrative center of the US Virgin Islands and its many shops tempt visitors with bargains in jewelry and other duty-free items. Beautiful beaches abound on St Thomas and the neighboring island of St John.

On the unspoiled island of **Tobago**, visitors can enjoy sunbathing, snorkeling, swimming at Pigeon Point, or a glass-bottomed boat ride to Buccoo Reef.

Tortola, the largest of the British Virgins, is a mountainous island of shimmering white sand and uninhabited satellite islands where a day can be spent on a secluded beach.

FAR EAST and SOUTHEAST ASIA

Hong Kong, a free port and bustling trade center, is the hub of banking and shopping in the Far East. Currently a British colony, it occupies Hong Kong Island, Kowloon Peninsula, and a mainland area adjoining Kowloon that, along with two bays and 235 offshore islands, was leased from China for 99 years in 1898. Hong Kong's waterfront, its famous skyline a jungle of gleaming highrises, bustles with marine traffic which includes traditional junks for ferrying visitors around the harbor. On shore the narrow streets are lined with food stalls, fortune tellers and bazaars. World famous for its shopping, Hong Kong is the place to buy designer clothes and luxury goods. A funicular whisks visitors to the top of the Peak for a sweeping view of the area.

Comprising four islands and many smaller ones, **Japan** is mainly mountainous with forested slopes, rushing rivers and fertile plains. A number of its peaks are volcanic, the most famous being Mount Fuji which last erupted in 1707. This perfectly formed, snowcapped cone is sacred to the Japanese and a popular subject for artists. Ports of call include Kagoshima on the island of Kyushu where passengers can visit Samurai houses and formal Japanese gardens, and Kobe, the gateway to western Japan. Nearby at Nara and Kyoto (former capital of Japan) are temples, shrines, gardens and shoguns' palaces. The shogun and samurai classes of feudal Japan were abolished in the late 1800s and Japan is today a modern industrial state and constitutional monarch. Its unique history lives on, however, in the Shinto temples, bonsai gardens and traditional kabuki plays.

The volcanic islands of **Indonesia**, which number in the thousands, stretch along the equator from New Guinea to the Malaysian mainland. Called the Dutch East Indies when merchant ships from the Netherlands dominated local waters during the spice trade, Indonesia gained independence following World War II. The islands' fertile soil supports 70 per cent of the population in agriculture. Bali, 'Morning of the World', is one of Indonesia's most beautiful islands. Its verdant hills are covered with terraced rice fields and the island contains numerous Hindu temples, banyan groves and beaches. The Balinese people are noted for their physical beauty, their gentle and artistic natures, and their uniquely ritualistic forms of music, folk drama and dance. No trip to Indonesia is complete without a visit to Bali.

Malaysian ports of call include Kota Kinabalu, situated at the base of Mount Kinabalu. Nearby at Mengkabone is a village built on stilts over the water. Pengang is one of nine states that make up Malaysia. Its capital of Georgetown contains street stalls, trishaws for hire, and gilded temples, not to mention the venerable Eastern & Oriental Hotel and other British colonial architecture.

Highly-regulated **Singapore**, located off the southern tip of the Malay Peninsula, is clean and crime free. Purchased by the British East India Company in 1819 through the efforts of Sir Thomas Raffles, this island republic and commercial center of Southeast Asia is an eclectic mix of Arabian bazaars, Hindu and Buddhist temples, and Victorian government buildings. Its five-star hotels, modern office towers and luxurious shopping malls are in contrast to such historical attractions as the Long Bar at the Raffles Hotel or the painstaking restoration of Chinatown.

The **Kingdom of Thailand,** formerly called Siam, retained its independence during European colonization of the 19th century. Laem Chabang is the port for the capital of Bangkok with its walled Grand Palace – a massive complex of gilded temples and shrines. Thai silk is a popular shopping item and one of Thailand's most memorable images is that of graceful Thai dancers in their bejewelled costumes and ornate headdresses. Other attractions are Phuket (the 'Pearl of Siam'), the elegant resorts at Pansea beach, and the country's tidy villages, each one dominated by a temple.

HAWAII / SOUTH PACIFIC /AUSTRALIA

The exotic islands that lie scattered across the Pacific Ocean have long attracted wanderlust voyagers, and today's cruise travelers can retrace the routes of seafaring explorers, most notably Britain's James Cook, who first charted these remote waters.

The world's cruise destinations include grand cities famous for their natural setting and cultural vibrancy.
Above – Hong Kong's harbor viewed from Victoria Peak
Opposite – San Francisco's Bay Bridge
Below – Venice, Italy

Above – Vancouver, Canada, its beautiful harbor backed by coastal mountains, is the base port for Alaska cruises.
Opposite – Amsterdam, an historic city of canal-lined streets, is a popular port for European cruises.
Below – Willemstad, Curacao, is a Dutch flavored Caribbean port famous for its shopping and golden liqueurs.

Whether your vacation choice is the 'Emerald Isle' of Ireland, the tropical islands of the Caribbean, or the castles and cathedrals of Europe – all can be visited by cruise ship.

Above – Bantry Bay, Ireland
Opposite – St Croix, US Virgin Islands
Below – Cherbourg, France

The smaller ports of call are often charming and scenic.
Above – Ketchikan, Alaska Below – Tortola, British Virgin Islands

Hawaii

The lush and volcanic Hawaiian Islands consist of deep canyons, fern grottos and sun-baked beaches of white, golden and black sand. Oahu's hub of Honolulu is famous for hotel-lined Waikiki Beach and such out-of-town attractions as Pearl Harbor and the unspoiled valleys of Waimea Falls Park. The former whaling town of Lahaina on the island of Maui is a port that provides access to some of the islands' best beaches and golf courses.

South Pacific

A member of the Commonwealth, **Fiji** consists of more than 800 islands, only 100 or so of them inhabited. In addition to the islands' beautiful white beaches and turquoise lagoons, ceremonial displays include the changing of the guard at Government House and the native custom of fire walking.

Perched on the edge of Mariana's Trench (the world's deepest ocean trench), the mountainous **Mariana Islands** are covered with impenetrable jungle and include the former Spanish possession of Guam, which is now American and was a key strategic base during the Vietnam War.

The twin islands of **New Zealand** contain extraordinarily diverse scenery – jagged peaks, fjord-like sounds, rolling hills and sheep-grazing plains, not to mention Rotorua's surreal landcape of volcanic thermal activity which includes spurting geysers and bubbling pools of mud. **Auckland**, located on the North Island, is New Zealand's largest city. Situated on a hilly peninsula and built around 60 extinct volcanoes, Auckland is cosmopolitan in atmosphere with pierside bars and restaurants overlooking the yacht-filled harbor.

The South Island's city of **Christchurch** (accessed from the port of Lyttelto) is situated on the River Avon and is British in flavor with stately buildings, a Victorian gothic cathedral, cottage gardens and antique shops.

The volcanic islands of **Samoa** have attracted writers such as Somerset Maugham who used Pago Pago as the setting for 'Rain', and Robert Louis Stevenson, author of *Treasure Island*, who spent the final years of his life here and was buried on Mt. Vaea 'under the wide and starry sky.'

Remote and beautiful, the **Solomon Islands'** golden beaches were the site of fierce fighting during WWII when American and Japanese troops clashed on Guadalcanal.

Australia

The only continent occupied by a single nation, Australia was claimed by Captain James Cook in 1770. A few years later, the country's first British settlement – a penal colony – was established on the east coast near where

Sydney now stands. Today most of Australia's major cities are located along this coastline of beautiful beaches. Lying offshore is the Great Barrier Reef – largest coral reef in the world. It comprises hundreds of individual reefs, islets and coral gardens, and glass-bottom boats take visitors along the reef to view some 400 species of coral and 1,500 species of tropical fish.

Brisbane, the capital of Queensland, is a thriving young city of skyscrapers and colonial buildings. **Sydney**, Australia's oldest and largest city, is also the most vibrant with its world-famous opera house, local beaches that attract surfers and sunbathers, and interesting pubs and restaurants. The southern city of **Melbourne**, Australia's cultural capital, contains three universities, numerous parks and tram cars.

Fremantle, on the southwest coast, has Victorian pubs, hotels and shops, and is the gateway to **Perth**, located six miles inland on the banks of the Swan River. This is wine-growing country as well as the place where Swan Lager is brewed. Cahunu Park is a good place to see kangeroos and koalas – animal species unique to Australia.

MEDITERRANEAN

The Mediterranean is referred to as the cradle of civilization and its name is a Latin word meaning 'sea in the midst of lands'. Ancient empires flourished and fell on the shores of this inland sea, leaving behind archaeological sites that today fascinate modern travelers.

The sunny Med, bordered by three continents, is chiefly divided into four smaller seas: the Tyrrhenian, Adriatic, Ionian and Aegean. The largest rivers flowing into it are the Po, Rhone, Ebro and Nile. The Mediterranean's variety of destinations – each rich in history, art and culture – combined with the region's natural beauty and warm, dry climate is what makes it the second most popular cruise destination in the world.

Egypt

The ancient city of **Alexandria** is the gateway to Egypt and port of access for Cairo. Located at the mouth of the Nile, Alexandria was founded in 332 BC by Alexander the Great and became a great center of culture. Under his orders the island of Pharos was connected to the mainland by a mole. Ptolemy II oversaw completion of the celebrated lighthouse on Pharos, where it stood as one of the Seven Wonders of the Ancient World until destroyed by an earthquake in the 14th century.

Cairo, the capital of Egypt, was founded in 969 AD. A port on the Nile River near the head of its delta, the city includes two islands – one of which is where the infant Moses was believed to be found in the bulrushes. A modern city with wide streets, Cairo is the largest city in the Middle East and Africa, with a population of over six million. Its historic sections contain famed mosques, palaces and city gates, and its many museums include the Egyptian National Museum with its ancient Egyptian art. Nearby are the Great Pyramids of Giza which were built during the Age of Great Pyramids (2680-2565 BC).

Nile cruises are an ideal way to see more of the archaeological wonders of Ancient Egypt. Additional ports of call include Luxor, located on the site of ancient Thebes, its great, pillared temple modified by a succession of pharaohs. Across the river, on the west bank of the Nile, lies the Valley of the Kings where the treasure-filled tomb of Tutankhamun, the Boy King, was discovered in 1926. Those who cruise the Nile, longest river on earth, also have the opportunity to ride on a camel or on board a felucca, the Nile's traditional sailing/rowing vessels.

Sharm-El-Sheikh, a Red Sea port, is rich in biblical history with its Monastery of St. Catherine (dedicated to the memory of the Burning Bush) and Mount Sinai, where Moses climbed to receive the Ten Commandments.

France

The shores of France have much to offer cruise passengers, whether their ship is cruising up the Gironde and Garonne Rivers into Bordeaux wine country or calling at the fashionable ports of Nice, Cannes or Marseille in the south of France. **Marseille**, its harbor lined with outdoor cafes and filled with yachts, is France's oldest city and was founded by the Ancient Greeks in 600 BC. The island of **Corsica**, bearing both French and Italian influences, has beaches of honey-colored sand and rolling, forested hills. Its main port of Ajaccio was the birthplace of Napoleon where his former home is open to visitors.

Gibraltar

Here the Pillar of Hercules was said to mark the end of the world by the Ancient Greeks. Visitors to this British crown colony can ride a cable car to the top of the Rock for a view across the Strait of Gibraltar to Africa. Another attraction is the Barbary Apes, living here in caves within a nature reserve.

Greece

This is a sunbaked land of mythical gods and goddesses, ancient ruins, and lively tavernas. On the island of **Corfu**, visitors will find miles of

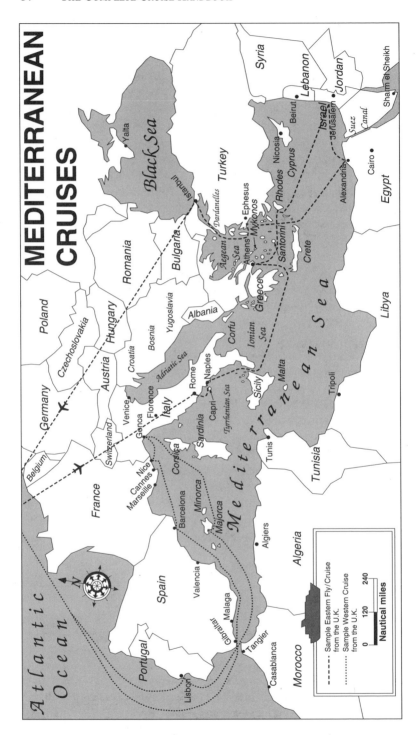

beaches and a countryside that is lush and green.

The southern half of **Cyprus** has everything you would expect of a Greek island – the tavernas in Limassol, the beach at Paphos where Aphrodite, goddess of love, was born from the spray of the sea, and the imposing castle at Kolossi.

Katakolon is the port for Olympia, site of the original Olympic Games when the warring states of Ancient Greece would declare a temporary truce every four years.

Piraeus is the port accessing Athens, Greece's capital and home to one third of the country's population. On the Acropolis overlooking Athens stands the famous Parthenon – just one of numerous ancient monuments found here. A funicular takes visitors to a restaurant atop Mount Lycabettus for a view of the Acropolis. Other attractions include local shops (selling fine leather and silver jewelry), tavernas where fresh seafood, dolmades and retsina can be enjoyed, and the Greek guards, in traditional dress, who stand outside the government building.

The walled city of **Rhodes**, on the island of the same name, was occupied by classical Greeks, Romans and Crusaders. The Knights of St. John built the massive fortress walls as protection against the Ottomans. Tours take visitors to the nearby village of Lindos, which consists of distinctive cubic buildings and contains the oldest temple in Greece. A swimming beach and tavernas are found at Faliraki.

The beautiful island of **Santorini** was formed by a volcanic cataclysm that is believed to have destroyed the existing civilization on nearby Crete. Cable cars and donkeys take visitors to the cliff-top town of Thira for a view of the harbor and your cruise ship lying at anchor.

Israel

Haifa is the port for visiting the Holy Land. The walled city of Jerusalem is sacred to three of the world's religions and is the site of the Wailing Wall, Dome of the Rock, and the 14 Stations of the Cross. Other places of interest are the towns of Galilee, the Church of the Nativity in Bethlehem, and the Dead Sea.

Italy

Center of the Holy Roman Empire and birthplace of the Renaissance, Italy is a vibrant country of vineyards, palazzos and artistic masterpieces.

The Eternal City of **Rome**, accessed from the port of Civitavecchia, is home to the Forum, the Colosseum, St. Peter's and the Sistine Chapel. **Genoa** also has museums holding great works of art. From the historic port of Livorno it's a short drive into the Tuscan hills to reach **Florence**, where the Medici Chapel and Uffizi Gallery contain famous works by Michelangelo.

Romantic **Naples** is situated on the edge of a bay, its surrounding hillsides covered with pastel buildings and the cone of Mount Vesuvius rising in the background. Attractions include the opulent Opera House, drives along the Amalfi Coast, excursions to **Pompei** – an ancient city that lay buried under volcanic ash for nearly 2,000 years – and boat trips across the deep blue waters of the Bay of Naples to the neighboring island of **Capri** and to the beautifully situated port of Sorrento, located on a peninsula separating the Bay of Naples from the Gulf of Salerno.

On the island of **Sicily**, its hills cultivated with vineyards and olive orchards, a popular port is Syracuse where ancient monuments include a Roman amphitheater and a cathedral built around the remains of the pagan temple of Athena.

Venice, one of the world's most romantic ports, is built on 118 islets between which run about 150 canals spanned by some 400 bridges, including the famous Bridge of Sighs. Gondalier rides are ever popular with visitors to this city of Renaissance churches and palaces which seem to float on the water.

Portugal

The capital of **Lisbon**, located on the Tagus River, has both a chic shopping district and an historic quarter of winding alleys and fado bars. The fishing port of Portimao, in the heart of the Algarve, is set among small coves and beaches backed by red cliffs.

Spain

A land of Roman ruins, medieval villages and Moorish architecture, Spain annually attracts millions of vacationers to its sunny beaches and pleasing countrysides of vineyards and orange groves.

Barcelona, site of the 1992 Summer Olympics, is located on the Costa Brava and is a city containing surrealistic architecture (Gaudi's Sagrada Familia and Parc Guell), ancient Moorish streets that are too narrow for cars, and the Ramblas – a shopping street of florists, stalls and cafes. The medieval port of **Cadiz** provides access to **Seville**, a Moorish city containing a tower, cathedral and palace of that era.

Malaga is the main port on the Costa del Sol and is overlooked by a hilltop castle. High in the mountains is **Granada** – the capital of Moorish Spain and site of the beautiful Alhambra Palace.

On the island of **Majorca**, amid olive and almond groves, is the cosmopolitan port of Palma set on a lovely, yacht-filled bay overlooked by a

Gothic cathedral. Out of town is the village of Deya where the former home of poet Robert Graves is located, and the Monastery of Valledemosa where George Sand lived with Chopin. Lord Nelson had a villa on the neighboring island of **Minorca**, overlooking the narrow, hedge-lined lanes of Port Mahon.

Tunisia

This Muslim country, with its wailing muezzins and street traders, is the site of the ancient city of Carthage, located near modern Tunis. Founded by Queen Dido, Carthage was the heart of the Carthaginian Empire and rivaled Rome as a center of power.

Turkey

Kusadasi and Izmir are the ports for Ephesus, an ancient Greek city with pillared porticos, statues and fountains. Antony and Cleopatra walked the marble streets of this 2,000-year-old city which was once a cultural center.

Istanbul, ancient capital of the Eastern Roman Empire, was called Constantinople until 1930. This fascinating city straddles the great Bosphorous Strait and is half in Asia, half in Europe – both physically and culturally. Famous landmarks of this city of mosques includes the emperor's palace, the magnificent church of Hagia Sofia, and the seemingly endless array of stalls in the Grand Bazaar.

MEXICAN RIVIERA

Mexico has margaritas and mariachi bands, fiestas and fireworks. It also has 2,000 miles of Pacific coast, often referred to as the Mexican Riviera. This region of rocky headlands, secluded beaches and holiday resorts is of Spanish heritage, evidenced in the port's town squares and mission churches. The narrow streets and open-air markets bustle with shoppers in search of bargains such as silver jewelry, pottery, embroidered cotton garments and other handicrafts. Bartering is part of the shopping experience in Mexico and this includes negotiating with a cab driver before setting off to see the local sights. Spanish is the official language and informality is the norm, with shorts and sandals acceptable street attire while in port. The pace here is relaxed, the sunsets are superb, and the local beers are excellent.

Los Angeles, home to Disneyland, Hollywood, Universal Studios and Beverly Hills, is the main port for Mexican Riviera cruises. Ports of call include Cabo San Lucas at the southern tip of the Baja Peninsula, Puerto Vallarta – a quiet fishing port until *The Night of the Iguana* was filmed here in 1963 and Richard Burton, accompanied by Elizabeth Taylor, made it a popular tourist destination – and **Acapulco**, one of the world's most famous resorts.

Set on a beautiful bay backed by mountains that are lushly vegetated with palm trees, Acapulco has long been a favorite haunt of wealthy vacationers, among them John and Jackie Kennedy who honeymooned here at a private villa. Acapulco was founded by Spanish explorers in the 1500s and its old quarter contains cathedrals and market squares while its new section is where the luxury hotels and designer boutiques are located. At La Quebrada cliff divers plunge 130 feet into a narrow inlet of the sea. Deepsea fishing charters are also popular in Acapulco, as are its championship golf courses.

NEW ENGLAND & EASTERN CANADA

North Americans can experience a taste of Europe without crossing the Atlantic when they take a cruise along the eastern seaboard of Canada and the United States. European settlement began in the 16th century with the arrival of Spanish, French, British and Dutch explorers. This region is being discovered anew by cruise passengers whose ships call at historic harbors and picturesque fishing ports. Summer and fall are the seasons for cruising this area, when balmy breezes and sunny skies prevail. The 'fall foliage' cruises are especially popular when autumn leaves add a brilliant splendor to the landscape.

Cruises along Canada's St. Lawrence Seaway include historic **Quebec City**, cosmopolitan **Montreal** and the scenic Gaspé Peninsula where wave action has chiseled the dramatic landmark of Percé Rock. Montreal was founded by French settlers in 1642 and the city's historic section, overlooking the water near the cruise ship dock, consists of cobblestone streets and the neo-Gothic Notre Dame Basilica. Quebec City is the only walled city in North America and a stroll along its narrow, winding streets is a step back in time to the 17th century when it was the capital of New France. Cruise passengers disembark at the foot of cliffs that were scaled in 1759 by British soldiers sent to conquer France's colonial fortress. The narrow streets are lined with shops and French restaurants housed in buildings that are three centuries old.

While France was settling eastern Canada, Britain began establishing colonies to the south after Sir Walter Raleigh – a dashing Elizabethan adventurer – landed on the shores of the New World and named the immediate area Virginia in honour of Queen Elizabeth I, the Virgin Queen. Small communities of British settlers gradually took root and now comprise some of America's oldest cities. The northeastern states are still collectively called New England, and popular ports of call include

New York, with its famous skyline, is still the base port for trans-Atlantic sailings as well as loop cruises to Bermuda.

Maine's **Bar Harbor** – a famous 19th-century resort for the wealthy who owned elegant summer cottages here – and **Boston**, with its numerous historical sites including the house of Paul Revere – a rebel leader and courier in the American Revolution who was immortalized for his 'midnight ride' in a poem by Longfellow. **Newport**, on Rhode Island, was a famous 19th-century resort with its palatial mansions.

New York, a major seaport since its Dutch founding in 1624, is one of the world's great cities for culture, cuisine and famous landmarks such as the Empire State Building and the Statue of Liberty. Further south, colonial America can be revisited on cruises that call at **Williamsburg**, Virginia (settled in 1632), Charleston, South Carolina (scene of the first incident of the Civil War in 1861), and Savannah, Georgia which boasts find old homes and shady streets.

NORTH AMERICAN RIVER CRUISES

North America's river systems, with their natural beauty and frontier history, now rival the popular European river routes for attracting cruise travelers. Modern vessels, many classically designed as replica steamboats, transport passengers in comfort and elegance along the continent's great waterways. The **Mississippi, Columbia** and **St Lawrence** are just some of the river systems included in various itineraries.

The Delta Queen gently rolls out of an Ohio River Lock while her passengers relive, in grand style, the steamboat days of Mark Twain.

Several paddlewheelers ply America's heartland on cruises that vary from three to 16 days. The Mississippi, Arkansas, Tennessee, Ohio and Cumberland rivers can all be traveled in stately grace. On-board lecturers enlighten passengers about the region's past with its historic Civil War sites, Southern mansions and Mark Twain connections.

Vessels that ply the Columbia and Snake rivers of Oregon, Washington and Idaho take passengers on a journey through the American west with opportunities to explore the region's remote canyons and gorges. A summer cruise of Eastern Canada's St Lawrence/Ottawa Rivers, from four to six nights in length, includes historic Quebec City.

PANAMA CANAL

One of the world's great engineering feats, the Panama Canal took more than 20 years to build at a cost of thousands of lives and was completed in 1914. Its opening marked the end of the centuries-old inconvenience in which ships had to round treacherous Cape Horn at the southern tip of South America to get from the Atlantic to the Pacific Ocean.

Vessels making the eight-hour transit through the Canal's six massive locks are raised and lowered 85 feet. The canal's operators have a scale working model of the locks in their control tower to ensure each lock is performing as it should. Another attraction of transiting the Panama Canal is the crossing of island-dotted **Gatun Lake** where passengers have the opportunity to view tropical plants and exotic wildlife.

As long ago as 1524, King Charles V of Spain ordered a survey of the Isthmus of Panama to determine the feasibility of a faster, safer route for sailing ships. The French public underwrote the first major effort at building a canal in 1881 by attempting to dredge a sea-level trench. Headed by Ferdinand de Lesseps, builder of the Suez Canal, this was a financial disaster and a national tragedy for France. It is estimated that 20,000 lives were lost during the French years at the Canal – almost all from disease. Thousands of middle-class investors lost their life savings as a result of the collapse of the Lesseps company.

A successful attempt to build the canal wasn't launched until 1904 when US President Teddy Roosevelt led the drive to take over the task. American construction of the canal commenced on land leased from the newly created Republic of Panama, previously a state of Columbia.

This land, called the Panama Canal Zone, extends for five miles on either side of the canal. Although the surrounding terrain of low, lush hills is a pleasing sight for cruise passengers, it was a dangerous breeding ground for malaria and yellow fever before the US military cleared miles of brush and drained swamps to eliminate swarms of disease carrying mosquitoes. Because of slides, especially in the area of the Culebra Cut, the canal requires ongoing dredging.

The canal was managed by the US until 1979 when it was turned over to Panama under the terms of a treaty. In the year 2000, control of the canal will transfer to Panama for the canal's neutral operation. Popular ports of call near the Panama Canal include Costa Rica's **Puerto Caldera**, where passengers disembark to travel inland to the capital city of **San Jose**, which is set on a plateau 3,800 feet above sea level.

Costa Rica's volcanic mountains, lush valleys and virgin tropical rainforests support such an abundance of flora and fauna that nearly one quarter of its total land area is preserved within national parks or reserves. One of Latin America's most politically stable nations, Costa Rica has a democratic government, no army, good roads and safe drinking water. Its Spanish heritage dates back to 1563 when Spain's conquest of this region began.

SCANDINAVIA & THE BALTIC

With beautiful, bold scenery and clean cities set on the edge of the sea, Scandinavia is an appealing cruise destination. Cruise passengers began visiting Norway's fjords before the turn of the century and they are still coming. Conditions here are ideal for summer cruising, with the days lengthening the farther north your ship travels, and the warm ocean currents providing Norway's coastal cities and villages with a relatively

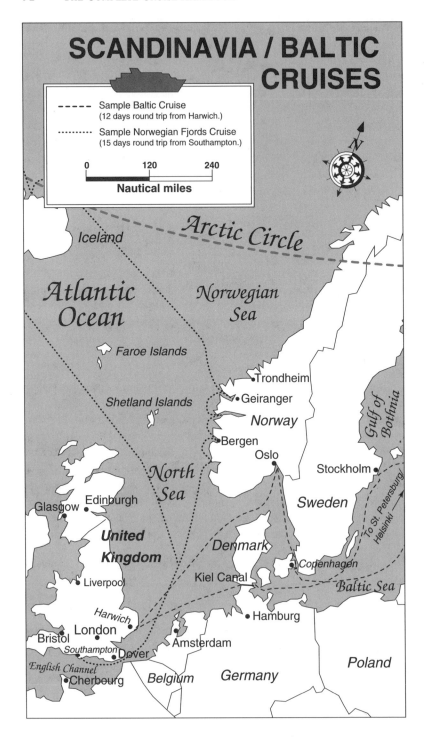

SCANDINAVIA / BALTIC CRUISES

- - - - - Sample Baltic Cruise
(12 days round trip from Harwich.)

· · · · · · · Sample Norwegian Fjords Cruise
(15 days round trip from Southampton.)

0   120   240
Nautical miles

Iceland

Arctic Circle

Atlantic Ocean

Norwegian Sea

Faroe Islands

·Trondheim

·Geiranger

Shetland Islands

Norway

Bergen

Oslo

Gulf of Bothnia

Stockholm

North Sea

Glasgow   Edinburgh

Sweden

United Kingdom

Denmark

To St. Petersburg
Helsinki

·Liverpool

Kiel Canal

Copenhagen

Baltic Sea

Harwich
London

·Hamburg

Bristol

Southampton   Dover

Amsterdam

English Channel
·Cherbourg

Belgium

Germany

Poland

warm and humid climate for a northern country. Bordering the island-dotted Baltic Sea are the capitals of Scandinavia as well as Russia's St Petersburg, built in 1703 by Peter the Great.

Denmark

Copenhagen, the capital of Denmark, has been a trading and fishing center since the 11th century. It's a charming city of harbors, squares and 18th century palaces, including the Danish Royal Family's residence. The statue of Hans Christian Anderson's Little Mermaid is a famous landmark, located on the waterfront near Langelinie Promenade.

Finland

In Finland, the golf courses are open 24 hours a day at the height of summer. The Finnish are famous for their fine craftsmenship, and the capital of **Helsinki** is a major shipbuilding port. The national art gallery and an opera house are just some of the cultural institutions to be found here, along with excellent Russian restaurants.

Norway

Ships cruising the fjords of Norway often anchor at the head of them where passengers can disembark for overland tours through pristine mountain scenery of alpine lakes, glaciers and waterfalls.

Ports of call include **Bergen**, where wooden buildings line old cobbled streets and, above the town, cable-car rides provide splendid views.

The port of **Geiranger** is nestled in a green valley at the head of a breathtaking fjord of sheer cliffs, cascading waterfalls and snowcapped mountains.

North Cape is the northernmost point of mainland Europe. Here you can stand atop 1,000-foot cliffs and see the Midnight Sun hanging just above the Arctic Ocean.

The modern capital of **Oslo** has impressive public displays of modern art as well as surviving medieval structures. Viking ships that date back to the 9th century are housed in a local museum.

Trondheim, founded in the 10th century, has a medieval stave church and old timbered houses.

Russia

St Petersburg (formerly Leningrad) was immortalized by the great Russian writers Pushkin, Dostoyevsky and Tolstoy, and was one of the world's cultural centers in pre-revolutionary Russia. Home to the famous

Kirov ballet company, St Petersburg also has a university and numerous theaters and museums. Its historic architecture includes the baroque Winter Palace and Cathedral of Saint Peter and Saint Paul. The famous Hermitage museum was reconstructed in the neoclassical style and today contains one of the world's foremost collections of art. In June and July, twilight lingers over St Petersburg and is called 'white nights'.

Sweden

The port of Stockholm, Sweden's capital, is built on several islands and peninsulas. Founded in the mid-13th century on the site of a fishing village, modern Stockholm is considered one of the world's finest cities in terms of well-planned housing projects, broad streets and numerous parks. The city's historic landmarks include the Church of St Nicholas and the massive Royal Palace.

EUROPEAN RIVER CRUISES

Much of Europe's history was forged along the banks of its rivers. Empires rose and fell, famous leaders came and went, and all the while the rivers of Europe flowed from their mountain sources out to sea. Over

A cruise along the rivers and canals of Europe affords passengers an intimate look at the countryside, with leisurely stops at charming villages and wine chateaux. Shown here is a 6-passenger hotel barge operated in France by Fenwick & Lang.

the centuries, the landscapes through which they carved their riverbeds underwent many changes. Hillsides were cultivated, bridges were built, and cities were born. To cruise the rivers of Europe is to journey back in time, through the great ages, while enjoying the natural beauty of these timeless waterways.

Shore excursions are usually part of a river cruise package, with pre-arranged coach tours taking passengers to nearby sights before returning them to the cruise vessel. The rivers plied by these cruise vessels include the Rhine, Mosel, Main, Danube, Elbe, Rhone and Seine. A guest lecturer is usually on board to explain the local history and entertain passengers with stories about the famous landmarks. When the vessel is underway, passing sights include cliff-top castles, vineyard-covered hills and walled towns. And when the cruise vessel docks at a riverside port, the city sights range from Roman ruins to Baroque monasteries.

Amsterdam is a port of departure when cruising Holland's canals or connecting with a port on the lower **Rhine**. This city of canals and bicycles is the place to see the world's largest collection of Rembrandt paintings, a museum dedicated to Van Gogh, and Anne Frank's house.

The Rhine flows past such historic cities as Strasbourg and Cologne. **Strasbourg**, in the Alsace region of northeastern France, was founded in Roman times. Its location, at the crossroads of Flanders, Italy and central Europe, made Strasbourg an important commercial center. Ceded to Germany in 1871 following the Franco-Prussian War, the city was recovered by France in 1919 following World War I. Today Strasbourg is famous for its beer and goose-liver pate. **Cologne**'s history also dates back to Roman times, but its famous landmark – the largest Gothic cathedral in Europe – wasn't begun until 1248, its nave and two spires added (according to the original plans) in the late 1800s. The Swiss city of **Basel** straddles the upper Rhine and is one of the oldest intellectual centers of Europe, its university founded in 1460 by Pope Pius II. The city's medieval gates and 16th-century town hall are examples of the local architecture.

The **Mosel**, a tributary of the Rhine, wends in a southwesterly direction to the Germany/Luxembourg border which it traces before reaching its source in the Vosges mountains of northeastern France. Its valley slopes are covered with vineyards and dotted with castles. Ports include Koblenz, a 2,000-year-old city situated at the confluence of the Rhine and Mosel, where Ehrenbreitstein Fortress towers some 400 feet above the riverbanks. The scenic town of Cochem contains cobbled streets and half-timbered houses within the remains of its medieval walls. Trier, near the Luxembourg border, is one of the oldest cities in Germany. The main center of the Mosel wine region, it retains many of its Roman monuments including a fortified gate, an amphitheater and the basilica. Other historic attractions are its Gothic church and the house where Karl Marx was born, which is now a museum.

The **Main** connects the Rhine with the Danube, the Main-Danube canal having been completed in 1992. Points of interest on a cruise of the Main include a sidetrip to the completely preserved medieval town of Rothenburg-ob-der-Tauber and such ports of call as Aschaffenburg, Miltenberg and Wuerzburg, which contain Romanesque, Gothic, Renaissance and Baroque architecture. All of these architectural styles are found in Bamberg, often described as Germany's most beautiful city. Its early 13th-century cathedral is considered one of Germany's finest medieval buildings and the facades of its Old Town Hall are painted with frescoes.

County Cork, Ireland

The beautiful **Danube**, the great river of central and southeastern Europe, rises in the Black Forest and enters Austria at Paussau – one of the most picturesque towns in Bavaria with its baroque palace, houses and fountains. Downstream, in Austria's wine-producing Wachau Valley, are the breathtaking sights of Melk's treasure-filled baroque abbey standing on a promontory above the town, and the old walled town of Durnstein, overlooked by the craggy ruins of 12th century Kuenringer Castle where Richard the Lionheart was held prisoner. Austria's capital of **Vienna**, city of music and center of the Hapsburg Empire, is filled with grand palaces and cathedrals. **Budapest**, capital of Hungary, consists of two towns - Buda on the right bank and Pest on the left bank. United in 1873 and today linked by eight bridges, this beautiful city of palaces and parks was once a capital of the Austro-Hungarian monarchy.

An ascent of the **Elbe** begins at the German port of **Hamburg** – the nation's second-largest city and busiest port located near the mouth of the river which drains into the North Sea. An elegant, modern city and cultural center, Hamburg is the birthplace of composers Mendelssohn and Brahms, and its noteworthy architecture includes the baroque St. Michael's Church. The Elbe winds past such fascinating ports as Wittenberg, where Martin Luther's house is now a museum, and Dresden, once a center of German opera and famous for its baroque and rococo architecture, much of it damaged during WWII. **Prague**, situated on a tributary of the Elbe, is the final destination. Capital of Czechoslovakia, this scenic city's old section is an architectural treasure and was where Mozart wrote *Don Giovanni.*

A cruise of the **Rhone** is a journey through some of France's finest wine country, including Cote de Beaune, Cote d'Or and Beaujolais. At each bend of the Rhone valley is a pleasing landscape of vineyards and hillside villages. Ports include Macon, with its magnificent abbey and the opportunity to take a wine tour, and the bustling city of Lyon, one of the gastronomic capitals of France.

A cruise of the **Seine** runs between Paris and Honfleur on the Normandy coast. Stops along the way include Giverney – site of Monet's stone farmhouse and beautiful gardens – and Rouen, where Joan of Arc was burned at the stake, Flaubert was born and the famous cathedral that intrigued Monet was built.

Across the English Channel, the inland waterways of **Britain** and **Ireland** meander past Georgian market towns, thatched cottage villages and splendid country estates.

Cruise staffs are renowned for providing passengers with impeccable service and fine dining.

CHAPTER FIVE

CHOOSING A CRUISE LINE

The Cruise Lines and the Workings of a Ship

I n Chapter 2 the different types of ships and itineraries were described in general terms. This chapter explains the workings of a cruise ship, followed by a directory that profiles the cruise lines currently favored by North American cruise passengers, with a brief description of their ships and itineraries. This directory is not exhaustive but it does provide an introductory look at what the major lines have to offer. A glossary at the back of the book will clarify any unfamiliar terminology.

THE SHIP

Something exciting happens on boarding a ship. The imagination is stirred by a strange yet familiar sense of nostalgia – a feeling, some will say, of romance. Many people, beginning with their first cruise, are smitten with shipboard life and never get it out of their systems. A ship has everything a great hotel has and something more: movement. Gliding across the sea, cruise ships can approach the most exotic and remote locations in safety, comfort and tranquility.

The grand ocean liners of the past were elegant and breathtaking inside, and graceful and inspiring to gaze upon from shore. A large raked bow, modest stern and creative finish to the funnel were the distinctive marks of the classic ships. Although some design features have been modified over the years as naval architects incorporate new materials and formulas into their blueprints, the romance and excitement of shipboard travel remains intact.

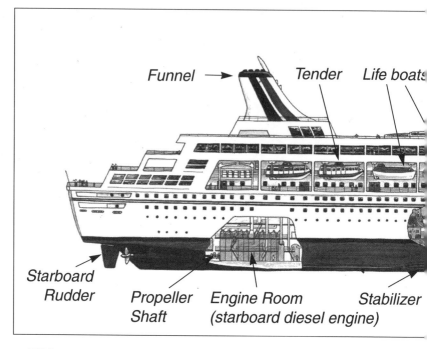

Funnel → Tender Life boats

Starboard
Rudder Propeller Engine Room Stabilizer
Shaft (starboard diesel engine)

While passengers, unconcerned with the logistics of running a ship, enjoy the comforts and luxury provided them, the **captain** and his crew are working around the clock to ensure a smooth, safe passage. It is from the **bridge,** located at the **bow** (or front) of the ship, that the captain and officers oversee the ship's operation using an array of computerized instrumentation.

How Ships Move

Making ships as maneuverable as they now are requires a great deal of power, delivered quickly and smoothly. To accomplish this, engines on most cruise ships run at a constant speed that produces optimum power. The bridge crew can tap into any amount of that power by moving small levers that turn the angle (or pitch) of the propeller blades. The angle at which the blades are set determines the speed of the ship.

Ships are pushed through the water with the turning of propellers, two of which are usually used on cruise ships. A propeller is like a screw threading its way through the sea, pushing water away from its pitched blades. Props can be 15 to 20 feet in diameter on large cruise ships and normally turn at 100 to 150 revolutions per minute.

It takes a lot of horsepower – about 30,000 on a large ship – to turn these propellers, and almost all cruise ships use diesel engines to do the work. It's the job of the **chief engineer** and his crew to keep these

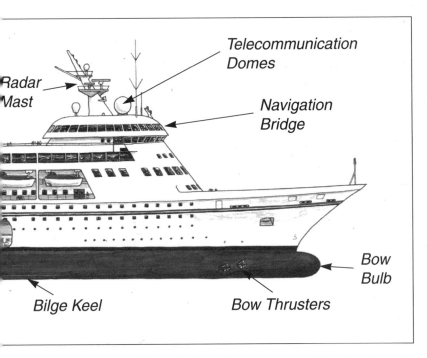

Radar Mast

Telecommunication Domes

Navigation Bridge

Bilge Keel

Bow Thrusters

Bow Bulb

engines running efficiently. In addition to propelling the ship, the engines generate electrical power for the rest of the ship. Gauges, meters and control panels monitor the various systems that keep hot and cold water flowing to your cabin, lights working, the radio and television playing, and heat and air conditioning functioning. Computer technology has transformed the workings of a ship's engine room which, in addition to improving engine efficiency, also gives more control and information to the crew on the bridge.

The amount of soot and smoke from today's ships is a small fraction of that from ships earlier in the century. Up to the end of the World War II, steamships used vast amounts of coal to heat large boilers placed along the length of the lower part of the ship. As a result, ocean liners of the past usually had two and sometimes three funnels to dispel the exhaust. (The *Titanic* had four funnels; one was a fake.)

More efficient steam turbine engines, introduced on ships after the war, replaced coal with diesel oil to generate the needed steam. Normally only one large funnel near the middle of the ship was needed to collect and disperse the gases. Diesel engines on modern ships transmit the power either directly through a transmission, which can result in some vibration felt throughout the ship, or by supplying electricity to large motors that smoothly turn the prop shafts. Steam-driven ships, a few of which are still in operation, also run very smoothly.

To turn a ship, one or more rudders are used. When a ship is moving, the crew makes a turn using the **helm**, which is shaped like a steering wheel and connected to the rudders by a hydraulic arm. Turning a ship with a rudder can be compared to turning a canoe with a paddle. The person seated in the rear of a canoe can turn it to the left or right by dipping the paddle in the water and holding it at an angle.

A ship's underwater appendages and innovations help the crew in different ways. Most ships have stabilizers, which are small wings located near the middle of the ship about 10 feet below the water's surface. The angle of the wings is constantly adjusted to minimize any rolling motion of the ship. A symbol (which looks like an upside-down question mark) is painted on the hull near the bow to show other vessels that might pull alongside the location of the bow thrusters in relation to the bow bulb. Thrusters have almost entirely replaced the use of tugboats for maneuvering the front of a ship sideways. The bow bulb reduces the bow wave, allowing a ship's hull to move more efficiently through the water.

Ship Size and Registry

A ship's size is determined by measurements that result in a figure called **tonnage**. There are approximately 100 cubic feet to a measured ton. Cruise ships used to be called large if they exceeded 30,000 tons and, while that still represents a big ship, most new ships are over 50,000 tons. The *Carnival Destiny* and *Grand Princess* – the largest ships ever built – are both over 100,000 tons.

Perhaps more important than a ship's size is the **space ratio** for its passengers. This can be determined by taking a ship's tonnage (usually noted in the cruise line brochure) and dividing it by its passenger capacity. This number is usually between 20 and 40 – the higher the number, the more space per passenger. A ship with a high space ratio can carry hundreds of passengers but not feel crowded.

At the stern of every ship, below its name, is the ship's country of registry. It may be surprising to note that your North American-based ship is registered in Monrovia, Liberia, Panama or the Bahamas. Certain countries grant registry to a cruise line's ships for a flat fee, without restrictions and onerous charges. Consequently, ships fly these 'flags of convenience' for tax reasons. Where a ship is registered has no bearing on the service and product on board.

The Role of the Service Staff

No cruise would be half so enjoyable if not for the remarkable service that passengers receive from the ship's staff. The **captain, chief engineer**, and

While the captain is responsible for the overall running of the ship, other officers look after specific tasks. Top – the captain keeps an eye on a difficult passage in Alaska; middle – two officers plot a course in the Caribbean; bottom – an engine officer shows the main controls.

their officers and crew, make up only a portion of total staff on board a ship. The majority of employees are engaged in transforming the ship into a floating resort hotel. This extensive service staff is overseen by a **hotel manager** (sometimes called the **chief purser**), who is second in rank only to the ship's captain. Reporting to the hotel manager are an executive chef, restaurant manager, food and beverage manager, cruise director, and purser. They in turn are in charge of departments that range from galley staff to housekeeping staff. This diverse team works in wonderful ways – many of which are invisible to the average passenger.

Most visible is the **cruise director,** who oversees the ship's entertainment. He or she usually has a background in show business and brings to the job a high level of energy and enthusiasm. Outgoing and easily approachable, the cruise director attends most social functions and is master of ceremonies at each evening's stage show. It's the cruise director's role to make passengers feel completely at ease and free to ask for any type of assistance. The cruise staff works tirelessly to ensure passengers are having a good time, all the while maintaining a cheerful disposition.

This goal of passenger satisfaction also applies to the dining room staff. Dinnertime is truly special on board a ship, with the the **maitre d' hotel** and his assistants lavishing attention on each passenger who enters the dining room. Waiters assist the ladies with their chairs and water glasses are promptly filled. That evening's menu is slipped into each arrival's hands and pre-dinner conversation fills the room, all in anticipation of the delicious meal about to be served.

While passengers are being pampered in the dining room, their cabin stewards are busy tidying and cleaning their rooms for the second time that day. No wonder some people don't want to disembark at the end of their cruise. It's always a bit of a shock to step back into the real world, where you no longer enjoy the special status that comes with being a cruise passenger.

Ships' Ratings

Cruise ships are rated annually by various cruise experts. While these evaluations are, by their nature, subjective, they do serve as guidelines in helping cruise customers determine whether a particular ship fits their travel budget and expectations. But before you zero in on a particular ship, it's best to familiarize yourself with the various cruise lines. Each cruise line has its own signature style which, for the most part, is found throughout the fleet. Yet ships within a fleet can still vary in price and rating, depending on each one's amenities, age and itinerary.

Generally speaking, a ship is rated according to its level of accommodations, facilities, maintenance and passenger service. Ships that offer the ultimate in comfort and personalized service are called **luxury-priced** ships.

Their atmosphere is usually described as 'formal' with passengers dressing up for dinner most evenings. These are also the most expensive ships.

Next in rank are the **premium-priced** ships, also called **upper-mainstream**. Their atmosphere is usually 'semi-formal' with men wearing a jacket and tie to dinner most nights. **Popular-priced** ships, also called **mainstream**, are more casual, with a fairly relaxed dress code in the dining room at dinner time and a stronger emphasis on shipboard activities than on elegant service.

Ships in the **budget-priced** category are often older vessels which, although comfortable, lack the sparkle of the newer cruise ships or the classic liners that are regularly refurbished to maintain their aura of luxury. This category has been shrinking in recent years due to stiff competition from cruise lines with newer ships offering comparable fares.

Regardless of the class of ship, the atmosphere on all cruises has become increasingly casual, especially during the day. In this directory, the **luxury-priced** cruise lines are indicated with five stars; **premium-priced** lines are given four stars; **popular-priced** lines get three stars; and **budget-priced** ships rate two stars.

DIRECTORY OF CRUISE LINES

American Hawaii Cruises ***

An American Hawaii cruise, with its excellent shore excursions, is a relaxing and rewarding way to visit all four of the Hawaiian Islands. The fleet consists of two classic liners, the *Independence* and the *Constitution*, sister ships of 30,000 tons which were built in the early '50s. The *Constitution* has the distinction of being the ship that carried Grace Kelly across the Atlantic to Monaco for her fairy-tale wedding to Prince Rainier. Both ships have a pleasingly Hawaiian ambiance created by the use of bright colors and local artwork throughout the ship.

Honolulu is the base port for 7-day cruises that visit the island of **Maui**, Hilo and Kona on the 'big island' of **Hawaii**, and Nawiliwili on the 'garden island' of **Kauai**. It's also possible to combine a 3- and 4-day cruise with a 3- and 4-day resort stay on one of the islands. Ideal for families with its casual atmosphere and 'free kids' program, the line also has theme cruises which include whalewatching during the humpback whales' winter breeding season.

Carnival Cruise Lines ***

The story of Carnival Cruise Lines is the sort of drama Hollywood would never touch because it seems unbelievable. A rags-to-riches tale, Carnival tore the lid off popular myths about cruising and introduced a generation of young people to the concept that cruising is not stuffy, but fun.

Carnival's informal party atmosphere attracts a high percentage of first-time cruisers – young and old, singles and families – who want to let loose on a holiday in the sun at an affordable price. Public areas are brightly decorated, cabins are spacious, and the entertainment is lavish. Extensive children's activities and facilities include Camp Carnival, where youngsters can be left with youth counselors while their parents go ashore at ports of call.

Celebration – 47,262 tons, 1987

Carnival Cruise Lines started operations early in 1972 with their first ship the *Mardi Gras*. The acquisition of this ship came from the timely rescue of Canadian Pacific's *Empress of Canada* by Carnival president and cruise line veteran Ted Arison.

The early years of Carnival were not without problems. Before the *Mardi Gras* left British waters to steam to Florida, British trade unionists tried to block her passage. Then, on her first cruise out of Miami she ran aground outside the port and remained stuck while Carnival's competitors sailed past. At one point in its first season *Mardi Gras* (now retired) arrived at a port of call running low on fuel. With little company money available, the casino slot machines were emptied of coinage to help pay the fuel bill.

The fledgling company was experiencing mounting losses when Arison completed a transaction to purchase Carnival. Shortly afterwards, the line's fortunes turned as the 'Fun Ship' image caught on and mass market cruising became popular. Arison soon added *Carnivale*, then *Festivale* (now both retired) to his fleet.

The Fleet

It was in 1982 that Carnival launched its first newbuild – the 36,674-ton *Tropicale*. Carnival was now reaching its stride of providing the right product for the right market at the right price. In 1985 the revolutionary *Holiday* was launched, turning the cruise industry upside down. Gone were the subdued colors and heavy feel of tradition, replaced with a radical layout which used bright lights, glitter and a thematic approach to the ship's public areas. *Holiday*'s theme is 'Broadway' with traffic lights, neon, street lamps, Times Square and a 1934 vintage bus.

The *Holiday* was followed by the *Jubilee* and the *Celebration,* similarly designed ships with bright vivid colors in the public areas, their respective themes being traditional British and New Orleans at Mardi Gras. The success of these ships provided the capital needed to acquire the prestigious Holland America Line and Windstar Cruises in 1989.

Miami-based Carnival has continued to expand its fleet in the 1990s with a stream of newbuilds planned to the end of the decade. Identical on the outside but featuring different and exciting themes on the inside, each of these ships features six decks of entertainment, recreation and lounging options, as well as a seven-deck-high atrium.

The first of these 70,000-ton megaships, each carrying 2,000 passengers, was *Fantasy*, launched in 1990 with a 21st-century theme. Sisterships include: *Ecstasy* (1991), *Sensation* (1993), *Fascination* (1994), *Imagination* (1995) and *Inspiration* (1996). Two more ships of the same class are planned for launch in 1998. The *Carnival Destiny* is the one departure, exceeding 100,000 tons with a passenger capacity of over 2,600. A sistership to the *Destiny* will be introduced in 1999.

Carnival's stimulating cruises attract the young at heart. Attractive features of the fleet's ships include spacious cabins. Shown above is an outside suite on the new Carnival Destiny.

Itineraries

Carnival offers various round-trip cruises including 3-and 4-day Bahamas cruises from Miami and Port Canaveral; 7-day Caribbean cruises from Miami, San Juan, Tampa and New Orleans; Alaska cruises in the summer; and 3- to 7-day cruises to the Mexican Baja out of Los Angeles year round. Carnival also offers Panama Canal cruises through the winter months out of San Juan.

Officers are Italian and service staff are International.

Celebrity Cruises ****

Few companies have so successfully reinvented themselves as Chandris Inc. did in 1989 when it started a division of ships with a new name and image to reflect a move to a more upscale market. Celebrity ships stand out with their striking dark blue and white paint scheme, fine bow and, on the funnel, a big X – which is the Greek letter 'C', for Chandris the parent company.

The cruise line has quickly gained a reputation for well-appointed ships and fine cuisine featuring menus prepared by award-winning master chef Michel Roux. Celebrity has consistently and successfully focused on fine dining for all of their ships. Vacationers seeking sophistication and gourmet cuisine will get just that. Celebrity's clientele tend to be affluent and in the 40-plus age bracket.

With the recent launch of the 70,000-ton *Century*, Celebrity now has four premium ships. Similar in appearance to the *Horizon* and *Zenith*, the *Century* is nearly 50 per cent bigger with a passenger capacity of 1,750. It

Zenith – 47,255 tons, 1992

features, among many innovations, a huge show lounge/theater which seats 1,000 people, a spa with picture windows at the bow of the ship, and a two-tiered dining room. Well appointed, *Century*'s decor includes cherrywood pillars and etched glass.

Celebrity's other ships include the 30,000-ton *Meridian*, launched in 1963 but rebuilt in 1990, and the 47,000-ton sister ships *Horizon* and *Zenith*, launched in the early '90s. A fifth ship, *Galaxy*, at 72,000 tons, is scheduled for completion in December of 1996. Celebrity's itineraries are mainly in the Caribbean, using Fort Lauderdale and San Juan as base ports. Celebrity also deploys ships to Bermuda and Alaska. Officers are Greek and service staff is International.

Celebrity offers its passengers a refined vacation at sea, with elegant ships and tasteful interiors. However, it's the cuisine that travel aficionados rave about and has resulted in Celebrity Cruises becoming a prominent success story of the industry.

Crystal Cruises *****

With only two 50,000-ton ships, this luxury-class fleet still manages to stop at over 150 ports around the world in a year. This is what money will get you – great service, gourmet cuisine, lots of space and a range of itineraries to excite any globe-trotter. The most exotic and remote locations in the world, from Anchorage to Zamboanga, are all possible with Crystal Cruises.

Crystal has built ships that are esthetically pleasing, both outside and inside. A finely raked bow, rounded stern and tastefully designed funnel positioned well aft give the ships a balanced look with a sheer-line the eye can actually follow. Inside, quality materials evoke luxury and elegance.

This Japanese-owned company began with the launch of *Crystal*

Crystal Harmony – 48,621 tons, 1990

Harmony in 1990, initally offering both inside and outside cabins. It discarded this idea with the *Crystal Symphony*'s launch in 1995, offering only outside cabins. Because these fairly large ships carry only 960 passengers each, there is an indulgent sense of spaciousness. Cabins are also large, ranging between 202 and 982 square feet.

As one would expect on such vessels, the food is gourmet quality and the menu selection prolific; special orders are available. In addition to the main dining room, there are two alternative restaurants – one Italian, the other Japanese. Officers are Scandinavian; service staff are European.

Cunard

This prestigious British line began operations in 1840 when Sir Samuel Cunard, a Canadian pioneer of regular transatlantic steam navigation, formed a fleet of four ships to deliver mail between Liverpool, Halifax and Boston. The Cunard *Queens* became the line's most famous vessels,

Royal Viking Sun – 37,845 tons, 1988

starting with the *Queen Mary* and followed by the first *Queen Elizabeth*, named for the Queen Mother while she was consort to King George VI.

Cunard's current flagship, the superliner *Queen Elizabeth 2*, is arguably the most famous cruise ship in the world. With a service speed of 28.5 knots, she is certainly the fastest. The rest of the Cunard fleet consists of a variety of ships, each with a different atmosphere, ranging from the ultimate in luxury and personalized attention on *Royal Viking Sun* to relaxed informality on Cunard's premium and popular ships.

The Fleet

Queen Elizabeth 2 *** to *****

The *QE2* was designed for transatlantic service but doubles as a cruise liner. Built in the UK, the *QE2* was launched in 1969 and measures 66,451 tons with 13 passenger decks. The ship carries 1,800 passengers and 1,000 crew. Passenger breakdown on transatlantic crossings is 41% British /40% American /19% other nationalities. Officers and crew are British; hotel staff are British and International. Currency on board is the US dollar except on European cruises where it's pounds sterling.

The *QE2* is extremely spacious with a high level of passenger service. Cuisine and degree of formality vary from dining room to dining room, which are allocated according to grade of cabin, i.e. Grill, First & Transatlantic class. The rest of the ship is open to all classes of passengers except for the Queen's Grill Lounge which is exclusively for the use of Grill -class passengers.

Notable features include a superb library, excellent children's facilities with supervision provided by English nannies, and a shopping arcade that includes a branch of Harrods. The interior decor has recently been modified from its original '60s style to the more traditional art deco look passengers might expect on a legendary superliner.

Itineraries: Transatlantic crossings from April through December. Year-round cruises to various areas, examples being Scandinavia, British Isles, Mediterranean, New England/Eastern Canada and the Caribbean.

Cunard Royal Viking *****

This luxury division of Cunard takes its name from the Finnish-built *Royal Viking Sun*, one of the highest-rated ships in the world. Extremely luxurious, spacious and ultra-contemporary but with classic appointments such as teak decks and walk-in closets in all staterooms, the ship carries about 750 passengers and 460 crew. Officers are Norwegian, service staff are European. Itineraries: Panama Canal, Caribbean, South America, Bermuda, Eastern Canada, Transatlantic, Scandinavia, Western Europe and the Mediterranean.

The luxury-priced *Vistafjord* and *Sagafjord*, each carrying 600 to 700 passengers and 350 to 400 crew, are medium-sized ships run by Norwegian officers and European/Asian service staff. Scandinavian decor and refined elegance are features of these classic cruise liners which offer worldwide itineraries similar to the *Royal Viking Sun*.

Cunard, well known for the QE2, enjoys a heritage of operating passenger ships on transatlantic crossings. The company operates a diverse fleet of luxury ships, such as the Sagafjord (shown here), which provide cruises to worldwide destinations

Sea Goddess I & II are highly-rated twin vessels offering yacht-like luxury with an intimate ambiance and personalized service provided by 90 crew serving 116 passengers. All suites are outside and passengers can dine in-suite whenever they choose, 24 hours a day. The dining room and other public areas are elegant and inviting, with a private club atmosphere. Officers are Norwegian, service staff European. In addition to a swimming pool and gymnasium, a water sports platform on the stern allows passengers to swim, snorkel, sail and ski right off the ship. These ships can maneuver into small ports and anchor off uninhabited islands. Their principal itineraries include the Caribbean, Far East and Mediterranean.

Cunard Countess *** / *Crown Dynasty* ****

The ships in this division are designed for the active vacationer seeking a casual atmosphere. These are mid-sized cruise ships with generous amounts of deck space and an easy-going ambiance. They cater specifically to the British market.

Stationed year-round in the Caribbean, the *Countess* carries 800 passengers and 360 crew. Her officers are British and the service staff is International. The ship makes round-trip Caribbean cruises out of San Juan, Puerto Rico. The *Crown Dynasty* is more upscale than the *Countess* but not as luxurious as Cunard's Royal Viking division. Her officers are European and Scandinavian; service staff is Filipino. The ship carries 820 passengers and 320 crew. It cruises the Western Caribbean and Mexican Riviera in winter. Summer cruises are to Alaska.

Dolphin Cruise Line **

Dolphin Cruise Line has transformed its fleet of older ships into floating family resorts. As the official cruise line of Hanna-Barbera cartoons, Dolphin's young passengers can look forward to rubbing shoulders with the likes of Fred Flintstone and Yogi Bear. Adult passengers enjoy the friendly atmosphere and fun activities delivered at a budget price. Miami is the line's main base port, from which passengers can embark on 3- and 4-day cruises to the Bahamas, and 7-day cruises to the Western and Eastern Caribbean. One ship is based at Aruba for cruises of the Southern Caribbean and Panama Canal.

Holland America Line ****

In business since 1872, HAL operated a successful service from Rotterdam to New York before turning to cruises in the early ' 70s. The company was one of the first to pioneer winter cruises to the Caribbean out of New York. It was also one of the first large ship companies to offer cruises to Alaska where it is today a major player, operating not only an extensive fleet of ships but a complete transportation and accommodation infrastructure for its numerous land tours. With over a century

spent operating passenger liners, Holland America is known for providing reliable premium service on its spotless ships.

Dutch officers and a service staff of Indonesians and Filipinos have helped build this solid reputation with a high standard of friendly service. Dark blue hulls and full wrap-around teak decks are standard features of all HAL ships. The generous use of wood and brass throughout each ship evokes a warm, traditional

Statendam – 55,451 tons, 1993

atmosphere. Each of HAL's ships have $1 to $2 million worth of art and antiques on display which, combined with the understated decor, creates an ambiance of relaxed European elegance. Fresh flowers grace both public areas and private cabins, adding to a refined ambiance which attracts a mature clientele. Cuisine on HAL ships is continental and consistently good.

The atmosphere on HAL ships is friendly without being familiar. It is also relaxed and pampered, with the Indonesian crew making passengers feel right at home and, although Holland America has a 'tipping not required' policy, most passengers do reward the excellent service they receive on these ships. While not billed as a line geared for children, HAL ships provide play facilities and activities, with extra counselors on board during school breaks.

The Fleet

The HAL fleet consists of eight premium vessels, including four new sister ships built in the '90s. The company's flagship is the *Rotterdam* - a classic ocean liner launched in 1959. The sister ships *Noordam* and *Nieuw Amsterdam* were built in the early '80s, and the *Westerdam,*

Passengers relaxing after a workout on HAL's Maasdam can enjoy the view from the Ocean Spa's Juice Bar.

launched in 1986 as the *Homeric*, was acquired and stretched (i.e. lengthened) to its current size in 1990.

But it's the new *Statendam* class of ships, named after the first of these ships launched in 1993, on which HAL will be relying for future business. Four of these 55,000-ton ships have now been deployed on cruises throughout the world with the enthusiastic approval of HAL's loyal client base. With a modest passenger capacity of 1,266, these ships have one of the highest space ratios found on premium-priced ships. The *Maasdam*, *Ryndam* and *Veendam* were launched in each successive year after the Statendam. The standard cabins on these ships are comfortable, all with two lower beds (that can be converted into a double), sitting area and bathroom with shower. Higher-grade cabins have bathtubs, and 150 come with verandas. These new ships have a sliding roof over the main pool - quite handy on cool or wet days in Alaska - and this area of the ship has an airy spaciousness which makes HAL lido parties appealing to passengers.

Itineraries

Most of the HAL fleet cruises the Caribbean in winter, using Fort Lauderdale, Tampa and New Orleans as its base ports. In summer, most of the fleet moves to Alaska where Vancouver is its home port. One ship remains in the Caribbean throughout the summer (in fall it cruises the eastern seaboard of the United States and Canada) and another provides summer cruises to a wide variety of European destinations.

Panama Canal cruises are offered each spring and fall, when much of the fleet is in transit between Alaska and the Caribbean. The *Rotterdam* is also deployed on interesting 'grand voyages' through the South Pacific and around South America.

Holland America has also offered world cruises for a number of years and the *Rotterdam* is often assigned to this marathon voyage. Despite being over 35 years old, this ship has an intensely loyal following and HAL is keeping mum about the fate of the *Rotterdam* beyond the launch of a new ship, as yet unnamed, in 1997.

Majesty Cruise Line ****

This line, formed by the owners of Dolphin Cruise Lines, comprises a single premium ship called *Royal Majesty*. Built in Finland and launched in 1992, this mid-sized vessel measures 32,400 tons and offers its 1,056 passengers an elegant cruise experience on its 3- and 4-day winter itineraries out of Miami to the Bahamas, Key West and Cozumel. From May through October the ship embarks from Boston on 6- and 7-day Bermuda cruises. Majesty also caters to youngsters with an array of children's activities and facilities including a children's pool.

Most cabins on this ship are outside and about a quarter are non-smoking. Public areas are generous and well appointed, giving a elegant air to the short cruises offered by this company.

Officers are Greek and crew are International.

Royal Majesty – 32,396 tons, 1992

Norwegian Cruise Line *** to ****

Originally called Norwegian Caribbean Line, this company pioneered the concept of dedicated Caribbean cruising in the late '60s when it introduced the first cruise out of Miami on board a small, amenity-filled cruise ship called the *Sunward.*

Officers are Norwegian and service staff is International. Cuisine is a combination of American and Continental. Today NCL's mainstream fleet ranges from ultra-modern ships to the classic ocean liner *Norway.* With the exception of the *Norway,* which is semi-formal, the atmosphere on NCL ships is casual with an emphasis on activities and entertainment.

This cruise company specializes in sports theme cruises hosted by celebrity athletes, and the nightly stage shows are lavish, often featuring well-known entertainers and Broadway-style productions.

The Fleet

Norway, NCL's flagship, is a restored classic liner originally launched as the *France* and now dedicated to year-round Caribbean cruising. At 1,035 feet, she's the longest cruise ship afloat and one of the largest at

Windward – 39,217 tons, 1993

Norwegian Cruise Line operates an eclectic fleet of ships, from the modern Windward to the classic ocean liner Norway (shown above) launched as the France in 1962.

76,000 tons. She carries 2,370 passengers and 875 crew.

Other ships in the NCL fleet include the *Seaward*, launched in 1988 and carrying over 1,500 passengers, and the sister ships *Dreamward* and *Windward*, launched in 1992 and 1993, and each carrying 1,242 passengers and 483 crew. Their contemporary design incorporates a great deal of terracing and glass to allow maximum viewing of the passing scenery. They all have a wrap-around promenade deck and good fitness facilities.

Recent additions to NCL's fleet include the *Norwegian Crown,* formerly the *Crown Odyssey,* which was launched in 1988 and carries 1,052 passengers in roomy and attractive surroundings, including a wrap-around promenade deck. The *Leeward,* refurbished in 1995, is a mid-sized ship carrying 950 passengers. Sleek and modern, the ship contains comfortable staterooms and panoramic windows in the public areas. It makes short cruises out of Miami, including private charters.

Itineraries

NCL's Caribbean itineraries include 7-day cruises out of San Juan, Fort Lauderdale and Miami, and 4-day Western Caribbean cruises out of Miami. Also offered are 3-day Bahamas cruises; 7-day New York-to-Bermuda cruises; 3- and 4-day California/Mexico cruises out of Los Angeles; and 7-day Alaska cruises.

Premier Cruise Lines ***

The 'Big Red Boats' of this family-oriented cruise line are based at Port Canaveral where passengers can take advantage of vacation packages that combine a 3- and 4-night Bahamas cruise with three days in Orlando visiting the Disney theme parks. The Premier fleet consists of two mid-sized, renovated ships called the *Star /Ship Oceanic* and *Star/Ship Atlantic*. Holding close to 1,600 passengers, these ships are not terribly spacious but do enjoy a high level of cheerfulness and energy, with non-stop activities to keep junior passengers occupied.

Princess Cruises *** to ****

Based in Los Angeles and purchased by P&O Cruises in 1974, this company doubled its fleet in the summer of 1988 when it acquired Sitmar Cruises, an upmarket Italian line. Today Princess operates nine ships and has been an industry leader in its ongoing introduction of new ships that are large, roomy and innovative in design.

Princess provides a consistently high level of service (about one crew member for every two passengers) throughout its diverse fleet of ships. Cabins are generally large, with twin beds that can usually convert to doubles.

Depending on the ship, officers are British or Italian and crew is European or International. The Sitmar influence is apparent in the fresh Italian pastas served in the dining room and the pizzerias where passengers can enjoy a quick, casual meal.

Crown Princess – 70,000 tons, 1990

The Fleet

The Princess fleet includes the sister ships *Crown Princess* and *Regal Princess*, megaships carrying 1,590 passengers and 700 crew. Their officers are Italian; service staff is International. The ships feature roomy cabins (which start at 190 square feet), all with walk-in closets, refrigerators and large bathrooms.

The *Star Princess* carries 1,470 passengers and 600 crew (Italian officers; European service staff). The cabins are spacious and well-appointed, and the ship contains playroom facilities for children.

The recent launch of the Sun Princess indicates Princess Cruises will continue to provide passengers with expansive public areas and spacious cabins. Shown above is an outside cabin on the Sun Princess.

The premium *Royal Princess* entered service in 1984 and was christened by Diana, Princess of Wales at the ship's home port of London. Carrying 1,200 passengers and 520 crew, the ship's officers are British and the service staff is International. All cabins are outside (a unique feature on a premium-priced ship) with full baths; public areas are spacious and elegant.

The *Sky Princess*, which carries 1,200 passengers, attracts a large number of mature cruisers. The ship's crew numbers 550 and consists of British officers and European service staff.

The mid-sized *Island Princess* and *Pacific Princess* (sister ships) are elegant and offer an intimate atmosphere popular with mature passengers. Both ships carry 610 passengers and 350 crew. Officers are British; service staff is International.

The *Sun Princess* is the newest addition to the Princess fleet, entering service in December 1995. The world's largest cruise ship at the time of her launching, this 77,000 ton megaship, and her sistership *Dawn Princess* (planned for launch in 1997), are attractive ships with a fine bow and a huge funnel enclosure which also shelters a tennis court. These two ships each have over 400 cabins with verandas as well as wrap-around teak decks. These ships also feature two four-deck atrium lobbies. Each carries 1,950 passengers.

Itineraries

The Princess fleet cruises worldwide, with a strong presence in the Caribbean and in Alaska – where it is a major player.

Caribbean cruises feature a day anchored off a private beach hideaway on Eleuthera in the Bahamas or on Mayreau in the Grenadines. Caribbean vacations can be extended with pre-cruise resort stays, one example being Walt Disney World in Orlando.

Alaska cruises are from Vancouver and San Francisco. Pre-and post-cruise land tours include coach/rail tours of Alaska (where Princess has its own land-based infrastructure) and the Canadian Rockies.

Mediterranean cruises are from the base ports of Rome, Athens, Barcelona and Venice. Other itineraries include the Panama Canal, Mexican Riviera, Spain and Morocco, Scandinavia, Europe and the British Isles.

Radisson Seven Seas Cruises *****

This Finnish-founded company, managed by Radisson Hotels International, operates three distinctly different luxury ships. The *Radisson Diamond* was built using revolutionary design technology and looks like a catamaran with its superstructure riding above the water on two submerged hulls. The ship carries 354 passengers who can enjoy panoramic sea views from an eight-deck lounge while cruising the Caribbean in winter and the Mediterranean in summer. The fleet's other ships are the traditional, 170-passenger *Song of Flower* – highly acclaimed for its interesting itineraries to exotic locations – and the 188-passenger, European-style *Hanseatic* which specializes in adventure cruises – often to higher latitudes.

Rennaissance Cruises ****

This fleet of eight small deluxe ships was built in Italy and launched between 1989 and 1992. The Rennaissance V to VIII are slightly larger at 4,280 tons and over 297 feet in length. Officers are Italian and the service staff is European. Each ship holds about 100 passengers and offers cultural cruises to unusual ports and locales in the Mediterranean, Caribbean and other parts of the world. Rennaissance offers an intimate cruise without crowds but also without the facilities and entertainment found on bigger ships.

Royal Caribbean Cruise Line *** to ****

This cruise company was formed by a pair of Norwegian ship owners in the early '70s. Headquartered at Oslo but based in Miami, RCCL soon set the standard for Caribbean cruising with its fleet of new, sophisticated ships sporting raked bows, midship pools and the company's trademark Viking Crown Lounge that wraps around the funnel and provides passengers with a panoramic view – the perfect vantage for watching the ship pull away from a Caribbean port as the evening sun sets.

As newer ships were added to RCCL's fleet, most recently the sister megaships *Legend of the Seas* and *Splendour of the Seas*, their designs changed but some elements remain, such as the funnel lounge. The upbeat and casual atmosphere on board RCCL ships appeals to young, active travelers who enjoy both sophistication and lively entertainment. Families also enjoy the many supervised programs for various age groups, as well as the special children's menu, and the teen disco.

Sovereign of the Seas – 73,192 tons, 1988

The Fleet

The RCCL fleet includes the premium sister ships *Sovereign of the Seas*, *Majesty of the Seas* and *Monarch of the Seas*, each of which carry 2,276 passengers and 825 crew (Norwegian officers; International service staff). These handsome megaships have spacious and impressive public areas, such as a five-deck-high centrum lobby and glass elevators. As on most RCCL ships, standard cabins are compact, and contain two lower beds and a bathroom with shower.

The popular-priced *Song of America* carries 1,402 passengers and 525 crew (Norwegian officers; International service staff). The ship has spacious public areas, two pools, and an area of open deck.

The *Sun Viking* is the smallest ship in the fleet, carrying 714 passengers and 320 crew, and it offers a more intimate cruise experience than on the megaships. Cabins on this popular-priced ship are compact but comfortable, some with one lower bed and an upper berth, others with two lower beds or one double bed.

The *Nordic Empress* cruises year-round to the Bahamas on 3- and 4-day itineraries. With 1,600 passengers and 685 crew, this premium ship provides a good party atmosphere in a contemporary setting. The officers

RCCL attracts a wide market of cruisers looking for variety and a high level of service. The company has given detailed attention to all areas of its new ships as shown above in the shopping area of Legend of the Seas.

are Scandinavian and the service staff is mainly Caribbean.

The biggest change in the fleet has been the recent launch of the new megaships *Legend of the Seas* and her sistership *Splendour of the Seas*. Although these ships carry over 1,800 passengers, there is an easy passenger flow in the public areas and, with larger standard cabins, a sense of space throughout (space ratio is a high 39). Features include a seven-deck-high atrium and a glass elevator that whisks passengers up to the Viking Crown Lounge. On the ship's uppermost deck, at the stern, is an 18-hole miniature golf course. A still larger ship, *Grandeur of the Seas*, will top the RCCL fleet at 73,600 tons when launched in late 1996. Truly floating resorts, these are a class of newbuilds RCCL will be adding to its fleet almost to the end of the century.

Itineraries

Half of the RCCL fleet remains in the Caribbean year round. The rest of the fleet offers seasonal cruises of Alaska, Panama Canal, Hawaii and Europe. The company is trying a number of new cruising grounds and recently deployed *Sun Viking* to cruises in the Far East. Other itineraries include short cruises from Miami to the Bahamas; 7-day Caribbean cruises out of Miami and San Juan (shorter 3- and 4-day cruises are being introduced here); Bermuda cruises out of New York; Mexican Riveria cruises out of Los Angeles; Alaska cruises out of Vancouver; and European cruises from a variety of ports including Harwich in the UK.

RCCL has CruiseCombo programs for passengers who want to combine a cruise with a land-based stay at selected resorts. It also has a Golf Ahoy! program for passengers seeking golf excursions in Bermuda and throughout the Caribbean. Cruises to the Bahamas and Eastern Caribbean often include a stop at Coco Cay, RCCL's private island in the Bahamas, and/or at Labadee, a private beach resort on Haiti.

Seabourn Cruise Line *****

Seabourn, founded in 1987 by the Norwegian industrialist Atle Brynestad, operates three luxury ships, *Seabourn Pride*, *Seabourn Spirit* and *Seabourn Legend*. The company's goal was to set the standard for luxury cruising and, judging by the number of awards Seabourn has received, it appears to have succeeded. Spacious but intimate, elegant but unpretentious, Seabourn ships are 439 feet long and carry only 212 passengers each. With their all-suite accommoda-

Seabourn Pride – 9,975 tons, 1992

tions and white-glove service, these ships provide the ultimate in understated service, fine dining and a relaxed ambiance. There is a no-tipping policy in place, and facilities include a health spa, gym, outdoor pool, watersports marina, library and boutique. The line offers interesting itineraries that span the globe and often feature a special event, such as a private concert held in an exotic location.

Silversea Cruises *****

The *Silver Cloud* and *Silver Wind* are relatively large for the luxury small ship category, each measuring 16,500 tons and carrying close to 300 passengers. They combine the intimacy of a luxury yacht with some large-ship features such as a full-size show lounge and domed dining room. The atmosphere on board is formal but with plenty of athletic activities available, especially watersports while in port.

SAILING SHIPS

Out of the growth of the cruise industry have sprung a number of cruise lines specializing in tall-ship products. Although the degree of passenger involvement with the working of the ship varies, the cruise lines all have in common a friendly intimacy and sense of adventure. As with all small cruise ships, these vessels also can poke around smaller islands and enter shallower anchorages and harbors. Depending on the locale, the ships are under sail for 40 to 70 per cent of the time. Although accommodations on some may be a little more cramped than on the big ships, the experience of being on the deck of a large sailing ship is exhilarating and romantic.

Star Clippers

This cruise line has two authentic late 19th-century clipper ships working in the Caribbean, the *Star Clipper* and *Star Flyer*, and if yarding up the main brace appeals to you, this is the cruise line to book with. Besides providing an opportunity for some tall-ship sailing, these four-masted barkentine ships also provide ample time for water sports and shore activities. The decor on these 170-passenger ships is turn-of-the-century nautical; officers are European and service staff is International.

Windjammer Barefoot Cruises

The largest sailing cruise fleet in the Caribbean, Windjammer has been providing the tall-ship experience in these tropical waters for over 30 years. The line's five tall ships all have interesting histories and many were formerly owned by famous people.

Fantome, built in 1927 and once owned by Aristotle Onassis, is the flagship of the fleet carrying 128 passengers. Other ships include *Flying Cloud*, *Mandalay*, *Polynesia* and *Yankee Clipper*.

Itineraries range throughout the eastern and southern Caribbean and include many small islands off the beaten track, such as Petit St Vincent, Bequia, Mayreau, Montserrat and Tobago – depending on the wind. Cruises are six days to two weeks.

Windstar Cruises

This luxury cruise line has three sailing ships, each accommodating about 150 passengers. Windstar is noted for its fine cuisine and superb service which appeals to clients seeking 'soft adventure' with the bottle of champagne nearby. The three ships – *Wind Song*, *Wind Spirit* and *Wind Star* – are identical and have four Bermuda-rigged masts (ie. no square sails). As is usual with sailing vessels, some deck space is taken up with machinery controlling sail trim, but the passenger/space ratio is very high for this type of ship.

The atmosphere is casual chic and has inspired a loyal following of cruisers who enjoy the range of exotic ports. Itineraries include the Mediterranean, some out-of-the-way ports in the Southern and Eastern Caribbean, French Polynesia and trans-Atlantic (a 14-day voyage with 12 days at sea). Cruises range from one to two weeks.

Wind Song – 5,703 tons, 1987

EXPEDITION CRUISES

As eco-tourism and 'soft adventure' travel grow in popularity, so does the 'expedition' sector of the cruise market. The following companies have proven successful in filling this niche market.

Alaska Sightseeing / Cruise West

The person often cited for popularizing cruises and vacations to Alaska is chairman of this Seattle-based company, Chuck West. The original founder of Westours (now part of Holland America Line), he worked for various airlines before opening a travel agency in Fairbanks that specialized in sightseeing tours of the state.

Today he operates four small cruise ships with itineraries that offer eco-adventure along the magnificent coastlines of Washington State, British Columbia's Inside

Spirit of Alaska – 97 tons

Passage and, of course, Alaska. Passengers are taken off the beaten path into stunning fjords and quiet anchorages. The line also offers spring and autumn cruises along Oregon's Snake and Columbia Rivers, as well as 3- and 4-night cruises to California's wine country. These depart from Sausalito, mid-October to mid-November, and travel along the Napa, Sacramento and San Joaquin Rivers, taking passengers to some of the most beautiful and prolific wine regions of the world.

These ships carry 70 to 100 passengers. Cabins are all outside and the cuisine is classic American. Crew and officers are American.

Orient Lines

Founded in 1992 by British entrepreneur Gerry Herrod, this company's corporate philosophy is one of providing cruises to exotic destinations at affordable prices. The emphasis is on interesting itineraries, many of them designed as complete cruise-tours with distinguished guest lecturers and local cultural performances, so that passengers get the most out of the foreign ports they are visiting. This company uses the phrase 'destinational cruising' to define the type of cruise experience it offers.

The ship used by Orient is the *Marco Polo*, built in Germany in 1966 and extensively rebuilt in 1993. The hull has been ice-strengthened for voyages to Antarctica, the top deck has a helicopter landing pad, and Zodiac landing craft are carried on board for transporting passengers ashore at remote destinations.

A medium-sized ship at 20,502 tons and 578 feet in length, the *Marco Polo* also contains all the amenities you would expect of a modern cruise ship, such as a swimming pool, health club, show lounge and elegant dining room that serves five-course meals. Standard cabins contain two lower beds and a bathroom with shower.

Orient's various itineraries cover Southeast Asia, the Orient, Russia's Far East, Indonesia, Australia, New Zealand, the South Pacific, India and Africa.

Swan Hellenic Limited

In 1983, P&O purchased a London travel firm owned and operated by R. K. Swan, who had been operating Mediterranean cruises since 1954. Popular with passengers who like to combine learning with relaxation, Swan Hellenic's cultural cruises of the Mediterranean have retained their well-deserved reputation for providing intellectually enriching vacations. They offer interesting itineraries, and guest lecturers from Cambridge, Oxford and other universities are on board to give talks on the archaeology, history and culture of the areas being visited.

For years these educational cruises took place on board the *Orpheus*, which Swan Hellenic chartered from the Greek-owned Epirotiki Lines. Starting in the spring of 1996, Swan Hellenic is using its own cruise ship called the *Minerva*. This completely refurbished vessel (a former Russian reconnaissance ship) is Bermuda registered with a British captain and officers. The ship's passengers, about 300 per cruise, are treated to the traditional Swan Hellenic experience in a sociable and relaxed atmosphere. The all-inclusive fare covers shore excursions and site fees as well as port taxes and gratuities. Passengers also receive handbooks with maps, historical overviews and information on the ports of call.

Spice Island Cruises

These expedition cruises of Indonesia are on small ships carrying from 24 to 150 passengers. The emphasis is on exploration and recreation, such as snorkeling and scuba diving. Onboard lecturers share their knowledge of local traditions, folklore and the natural sights. The yacht-like *Bali Sea Dancer,* accommodating 150 passengers, sails out of Bali on 3- or 4- day excursion cruises to the Spice Islands. Two expedition vessels – *Spice Islander* and *Island Explorer* – carry 42 and 24 passengers each on 7- to 14-night cruises of Indonesia.

Special Expeditions

This company would have met the approval of Phineas Fogg had he decided to add even more adventure to his journeys. Founded in the late '60s by Lars-Eric Lindblad, it introduced expedition cruising to some of the most remote corners of the globe. The tradition of adventure continues with his son Sven and the company offers cruises on a number of ships which include: *Caledonian Star*, a 300-foot ship which explores the Far East; *Polaris*, which explores South and Central America as well as Europe, Scandinavia and the Arctic; and *Sea Bird* and *Sea Lion*, positioned in Alaska. The company also charters the exceptionally beautiful *Sea Cloud*, a famous four-masted barque once owned by the Post (cereal) family, for cruises of the Caribbean and the Mediterranean.

World Explorer Cruises

For many years this company operated the oldest steamship of the Alaska fleet, the ss *Universe*. The 500-passenger *Universe* was, however, retired in 1995, and World Explorer has chartered a Commodore Cruise Line ship, the *Enchanted Seas*, for its Alaska cruises. This 739-passenger ship offers more public space and speed than did the *Universe*, allowing it to add ports of call to its 7- and 14-day voyages out of Vancouver. The line continues its tradition of offering informal cruises with in-depth lectures about Alaska. A number of experts are on board each cruise to provide talks on wildlife, native culture and natural phenomena.

RIVER CRUISES

A river cruise, similar to traveling by train, provides a unique and mellow perspective on the passing scenery – whether it be the chateaus and vineyards of Europe, the pyramids of Egypt or the antebellum mansions of the American South. The vessels that ply the world's inland waterways range from small luxury barges for parties of six to vessels carrying close to 200 passengers.

American West Steamboat Company

This new cruise line debuted its first ship, *Queen of West*, in 1995. The *Queen* is an authentic sternwheel-drive of 230 feet and able to carry 165 passengers. Itineraries are along the Columbia, Snake and Williamette Rivers of the Pacific Northwest on cruises of 2- to 7-nights year round. The ambiance on board is turn-of-the-century with plush decor, fine dining and nightly variety entertainment similar to 19th-century showboats. Motorcoach shore tours explore the history of the West, the Oregon Trail/Lewis & Clark journey, and native American culture.

Delta Queen Steamboat Company

In 1857 a young man began his apprenticeship as a Mississippi steamboat pilot. The final phase of American continental expansion was nearly complete, and the civil war and industrial revolution were yet to happen. It is little wonder that Samuel Clements, a.k.a. Mark Twain, grew to look back on that time of his life as one of ecstasy.

As Mark Twain knew, there are few better ways to reflect upon life than while traveling by riverboat. The beautiful, eternal Mississippi sweeps by cities and towns in the heart of America where miles of shoreline have changed little from the days of Huck Finn. Delta Queen has tapped into this artery of nostalgia with three ships steaming the rivers of the mid-west on cruises of various lengths.

The oldest, the *Delta Queen*, was built in 1926 for 182 passengers and features late-Edwardian saloons and parlors, elegant dining rooms and a grand stairway of teak and brass. Its cabins combine antique furniture with modern amenities. The boat has been entered in the National Register of Historic Places and is considered an authentic, fully-restored masterpiece. The *Mississippi Queen* entered service in 1976 and the newest, the *American Queen*, was launched in 1995.

Itineraries include four regions and vary from 3- to 16-nights. The 'American South' tour cruises the lower Mississippi and Arkansas Rivers; 'Crossroads of America' traverses the Arkansas River delta along the Ozark foothills to Tulsa, Oklahoma or St. Louis, Missouri, with stops at Little

American Queen – 1995

Rock, Arkansas and Memphis, Tennessee. 'America's Heartland' takes travelers along the upper Mississippi River from St. Louis to St. Paul, Minnesota (gliding by Mark Twain's home town of Hannibal, Missouri); and 'Wilderness America' follows the Ohio, Tennessee and Cumberland Rivers along routes taken by America's westward-bound pioneers.

EuropAmerica River Cruises

This five-vessel luxury fleet, operated by Peter Deilmann Shipping, offers cruises of the Rhine, Rhone, Danube and Elbe Rivers of Europe. The majority of these cruises are seven days in length, with additional 10- and 11-day cruises also available. These 4- and 5-star vessels resemble floating hotels with an elegant dining room, boutique, beauty salon, library, and intimate lounges and bars. Staterooms are finely-appointed, each with a private bathroom containing a shower.

Fenwick & Lang

This division of Sunmakers Travel Group offers luxury barge cruises in France, England and Holland. Their all-inclusive 3- and 6-night barge tours are operated by a fleet of 18 deluxe hotel barges accommodating six to 51 passengers. They range from elegant all-suite vessels, including luxury charter-only craft, to those offering standard accommodations at budget prices. The canals and rivers of France's beautiful Champagne, Burgundy, Upper Loire and Provence regions can all be toured, with opportunities to disembark at various locks and bike along the towpath or explore a tiny canalside village before rejoining the barge a few locks down. French wine and cuisine are served at each evening's candlelight dinner. The English itineraries combine river cruising with visits to stately homes, thatched-cottage villages and the famous college towns of Oxford and Cambridge. Holland cruises are offered in spring, during the tulip season.

KD River Cruises of Europe

Since 1826, this German-founded cruise company has plied the rivers of Europe. Queen Victoria was one of many heads of state who cruised aboard a KD vessel, and elegant service is still a hallmark of these river cruises. Custom-built for river cruising, KD's vessels are fully air-conditioned with a bar, restaurant, reading room and gift shop. The observation lounge has panoramic windows and each vessel has an outer veranda and sundeck. Most vessels also have a swimming pool, sauna and solarium. Cabins are all outside and they range from deluxe, with two lower beds, minibar and TV, to standard, with upper and lower bed. All cabins have a bathroom with shower.

KD's itineraries include the rivers of Europe – the Rhine, Moselle, Danube, Elbe and Seine – as well as the river Nile. They range in length from 7- to 15-days, with optional extended stays at various great cities of Europe or in the Swiss Alps.

P&O's Swan Hellenic European River Cruises

From the North Sea to the Black Sea, the modern and spacious *Rembrandt van Rijn* offers its 90 passengers a relaxing journey along the scenic and historic waterways of Europe. All cabins are outside with twin beds and a private bathroom with shower. This three-decked vessel has a dining room, lounge, bar and partly-covered sun deck. Each cruise has a knowledgeable guest lecturer on board. Itineraries include 5- to 7-day tours of Holland and the Bulbfields; 11- to 15-day cruises of the Main and Danube; and 8- to 11-day cruises of the Rhine, Moselle and Main Rivers.

Thomas Cook's Nile Fleet

When the Englishman Thomas Cook founded his company in 1841 and created one of the world's most successful travel agencies, he was tapping into a growing market. Victorians were avid travelers and, it could be said, they were the world's first tourists as they ventured, often by ship, to far-flung regions of the globe.

In 1884, Cook sent an entire expeditionary force of 18,000 men up the Nile to relieve a British general and his troops who were under siege at Kartoum. Thomas Cook Holidays is still sending expeditions up the Nile but these are now on custom-designed river vessels. The

Thomas Cook Nile Fleet includes three new vessels – the *Royal Rhapsody*, *Royal Orchid* and *Royal Serenade* – all boast exquisite decor, spacious public rooms and expansive sun decks, both open and shaded. Cabins, which number only 27 including six suites, are all finely appointed with two beds, private bathroom with shower, and a large tinted window. On the upper deck is a swimming pool, jacuzzi and sunken bar. The overall ambiance is one of being on board a millionaire's yacht with a tour manager as host.

Another vessel used by Cook's Nile cruises is the *Eugenie*, named after the French Empress who opened the Suez Canal in 1869. Built in 1993, this ship's classic design and decor evokes the Edwardian elegance of yesteryear with such appointments as wood -paneling and mosaic floors. Modern amenities include a swimming pool and jacuzzi on the upper sundeck. Comfortable cabins, all outside, feature radio and music channels, and some have private verandas. A crew of 65 serves the *Eugenie*'s 102 passengers.

Fully-escorted Cook's Tours of Egypt vary in length from 6- to 17-days with the Nile cruise portion ranging from 3- to 10- nights depending on which tour is booked.

SOME OTHER LINES

For North Americans interested in cruising on board a ship that caters to other nationalities, the following lines merit consideration.

Bergen Line

Bergen Line has long operated passenger ferries on the North Sea routes. Today it operates close to 30 vessels, including those of Norwegian Coastal Voyage – an expedition-style cruise to remote towns and villages tucked among the stunning fjords of Norway. Bergen's growing Norwegian Coastal fleet will consist of 11 vessels by early 1997, over half of them built since 1993. The fleet offers year-round specialty cruises of the Norway coast, from Bergen to Kirkenes in the Arctic Circle. Cabins range from first-class suites to simple double berths, and the ships carry cars for tourists wishing to use the port-to-port service as part of a motoring holiday.

Costa Cruise Lines

This premium Italian line originated with transatlantic passenger service in the late '40s, then ventured into the cruise market in the '60s. By the early '80s it had expanded into a worldwide operation. Costa's Italian flair and festive atmosphere make it popular with Mediterranean cruisers. The ships in Costa's fleet are modern and elegant with contemporary styling and the use of classical Italian marble, hand-made ceramic tile and decorative murals. The officers are Italian and the service staff is Italian/International. Cuisine is predominantly Northern Italian. A number of Costa ships are ideal for families with their numerous three-and-four-berth cabins as well as such facilities as a playroom, supervised youth activity center and babysitting services, as well as inclusive children's fares.

The *Costa Romantica* and *Costa Classica*, sister ships, each carry 1,350 passengers and 650 crew. The smaller sister ships–*Costa Allegra* and *Costa Marina* – each carry 800 passengers and 500 crew. The Costa fleet also includes the spacious *Costa Riviera* (984 passengers); the medium-sized *Eugenio Costa* (1,158 passengers); and the intimate *Daphne* (422 passengers). The new 75,000-ton *CostaVictoria* is slated for delivery June 1996.

Currency used on board is the Italian lira for the Mediterranean and Northern Europe cruises, and the US dollar for North American and Transatlantic cruises. Itineraries include Eastern and Western Caribbean cruises out of Miami, San Juan and Guadeloupe; Mediterranean cruises from Genoa and Venice; and Baltic & Scandinavian cruises departing from Amsterdam and Dover, England.

P&O Cruises

This British cruise company began operations in 1837, the year Queen Victoria ascended the throne. Originally called the Peninsular Steam Navigation Company when running mail to Spain and Portugal ('the Peninsula'), the company expanded its service and became the Peninsular and Oriental, offering service to Bombay and Australia as well as cruises to the fjords of Norway, the Mediterranean and the Caribbean. Among those who embarked on P&O cruises were William Thackeray and Mark Twain. P&O is still one of Britain's favorite cruise lines, both for its affordability and the atmosphere on board its ships which – as stated in its brochures – is utterly British. North American bookings are handled by Princess Cruises.

The *Oriana* is P&O's newest ship and this superliner was specifically designed for the British cruise market. At 67,000 tons and 850 feet in length, the *Oriana* holds 1,760 passengers and 760 crew. British registered, the ship's officers are British and service staff are International. A one-class ship with all the facilities you would expect on a ship this size – three swimming pools, nine bars and extensive children's facilities – the *Oriana* also has some stunning features, such as a four-deck atrium with a cascading waterfall and spiral staircase. Itineraries are worldwide. *Canberra*, which entered service in 1961, is a long-time favorite with British cruisers. Well maintained with comfortable accommodations and excellent children's facilities, the *Canberra* is one class and appeals to the budget-conscious cruise traveler. Itineraries are worldwide.

Oriana – 69,153 tons, 1995

P&O's third ship, formerly the *Sea Princess*, was recently renamed *Victoria* in honor of a former P&O ship launched in 1887 to celebrate Queen Victoria's golden jubilee. A former ocean liner, the upscale *Victoria* is intimate and elegant with a decor dominated by fine wood paneling and rich fabrics. Her officers are British; service staff are British and Goan. The *Victoria* is smaller than the other two P&O liners, carrying 715 passengers and 380 crew. Her itineraries include Caribbean cruises out of San Juan, Puerto Rico, and Mediterranean cruises out of Malaga, Venice and Aqaba, Jordan.

Royal Olympic Cruises

In 1995, Epirotiki Cruise Line and Sun Line Cruises, Greece's two leading cruise companies, joined forces to form a new cruise company called Royal Olympic. Using the colors of the Greek flag to differentiate the two brand names operating under the Royal Olympic umbrella, the blue ships of Sun Line offer traditional cruises, while the white ships of Epirotiki provide a more relaxed atmosphere. The line features destination-oriented itineraries in the Mediterranean, specifically the Greek Islands, with plans to deploy a few of the ships each winter to the Caribbean and other cruising areas.

CHAPTER SIX

BOOKING YOUR CRUISE

A rmed with information contained in the preceding chapters of this book, you will be well on your way to choosing the cruise best suited to your vacation plans. This chapter will help you zero in on a specific cruise and provide guidelines on how to book it.

The first step is to visit a reliable travel agent, one who belongs to an official organization such as the American Society of Travel Agents (ASTA) or, in Canada, the Alliance of Canadian Travel Associations (ACTA). Better yet, choose one that is also a member of Cruise Lines International Association (CLIA) – an independent marketing and training organization for the North American cruise industry. Member agents of CLIA take courses, attend seminars and inspect ships, all in an effort to gain expertise in cruise travel. An agent with official CLIA accreditation (a Cruise Counsellor or Master Cruise Counsellor) can provide knowledgeable advice regarding the various lines, their ships, and which ones are best suited to individual clients. Other agents who specialize in cruise vacations may not have official accreditation, but if they have been in the business for some time they will have gained their insight through practical experience, which is invaluable in any field.

Simply asking a travel agent if he or she has taken a cruise is the first step to finding a professional and helpful agent – preferably one with whom you can develop a long-term and mutually beneficial relationship. In these times of shopping around for the 'best deal', it's important to remember that agents reward their loyal clients with good service, which includes informing them first of any time-sensitive discounts that come across their desk. And a good agent can match you with the right cruise line and ship – an important service because no one is getting a 'deal' if they're unhappy with their vacation.

The Agent

Many agents work with specific cruise lines and will naturally steer you towards one of these. This is not necessarily a negative for the consumer because agents are familiar with the cruise products they regularly sell and about which they receive constant feedback from clients. Also, if you make it clear what you want and don't want from a cruise vacation, an agent will be able to make an informed recommendation regarding the lines with which they regularly book clients. For example, agents that work closely with Carnival Corporation have at their fingertips the best fares and information on a wide range of Carnival products: popular-priced Carnival Cruises, premium-priced Holland America Line, luxury-priced Seabourn Line, and the luxury sailing ships of Windstar. Other agents may have developed strong ties with a mix of companies unrelated to each other and which cover the range of cruise vacations, from luxury class to budget travel. And should you have already decided on a particular cruise line, you can book the cruise of your choice with any agent.

When looking for an agent, feel free to wander into any travel agency – retail agencies welcome browsers – and ask whatever questions you might have about cruising. Don't worry about sounding uninformed – the majority of people know very little about shipboard travel and what a cruising vacation entails. A good way to get a fix on cruising is to view a video illustrating the size and space of modern cruise liners and the range of activities that can be enjoyed on board.

Cruise agencies are well stocked with brochures on various cruise lines. Take a selection of these home to leaf through at your leisure. The photos inside will give you a fairly good impression of the clientele each line appeals to and the atmosphere found on board. Jot down any questions you would like to ask your travel agent about a particular cruise line and/or cruising region.

The first question on most people's minds is 'What does a cruise cost?' Below is a rough guideline on the sort of cruise you can expect for the money you are prepared to spend. A number of variables enter into the equation, such as the type of cruise line, the grade of cabin, the destination, and the length of the cruise.

The prices quoted are per adult passenger, in US funds, and include on-board accommodations, meals and entertainment. These prices also allow for airfares, port taxes and transfers but do not include onboard purchases such as drinks or gifts. Early booking discounts (which range from 10 to 25 per cent, sometimes more), free cabin upgrades and special introductory or home port promotions are not factored into these quoted prices. Children's fares are lower if sharing a cabin with two adults, and infants under the age of two are sometimes free.

What you can expect if your budget is:

$1000 or Less:
Basic inside cabin on budget and popular-priced cruise lines. Vacation length of three and four days. Destinations include Mexican Riveria, Bahamas.

$2000 and Less:
Basic inside or outside cabin, sometimes better, on budget, popular and a few premium-priced ships, depending on destination. Vacation of 4 to 7+ days. Fly/cruises to the Bahamas, Caribbean, Mexican Riviera, New England/Eastern Canada and Alaska.

$2000 to $4000:
Better cabin selection – outside cabin (possibly with veranda) on budget- to premium-priced range of ships, depending on length and destination of cruise. Some luxury cruises available. Vacations of 7 to 10+ days. Fly/cruises to Caribbean, Alaska, Europe, Mediterranean. Some Far East and South Pacific fly/cruises.

$4000 to $6000:
Better cabin selection – outside cabins, some with veranda on a good selection of premium to luxury-priced ships. Vacations of 7 to 10+ days. Fly/cruises to major cruising destinations.

$6000 to $10,000:
Better cabins on the better ships are available in this price range, choosing from a good selection of premium and luxury-priced ships. Holidays of 10 to 14 + days with cruises to worldwide destinations. Some extended cruises of over 20 days also available.

$10,000+:
Upper-grade cabin selection on upper-end premium and luxury-priced ships. Cruise lengths of 14+ days; extended cruises (20 to 30+ days); round-the-world cruises of 90 days are in the $20,000 range. Worldwide destinations available.

Making A Decision

Once you have determined your travel budget, the next questions are ones you must ask of yourself: Where would I like to go? At what time of the year? For how long? You may already know what part of the world you want to see. However, if you're open to suggestions, Chapter 4, *Ports of Call*, may help with this decision.

The more popular the cruising region, the more choice there is in terms of cruise lines and lengths of cruises available. For instance, Caribbean cruises range from three nights to two weeks. Some of the popular cruising areas are seasonal while others can be cruised throughout the year. The Caribbean, its tropical heat tempered by trade winds, can be visited by cruise ship year round. December to April are the high-season months when the weather is most pleasant and visitors come to escape winter weather back home. For Christmas sailings, the major cruise lines, in addition to creating a festive on-board atmosphere, offer special Caribbean itineraries. Summer in the Caribbean is popular with families, when the kids are on school vacation. Late summer through fall is hurricane season and the cruise lines sometimes have to make last-minute changes to their itineraries to avoid an approaching storm or bypass a wind-ravaged port of call.

Spring through fall are the main seasons for cruising the northern hemisphere, areas such as the Mediterranean, Northern Europe, Alaska and New England/Eastern Canada, where 'fall foliage' cruises are especially popular. Spring and fall are also the seasons for repositioning cruises. These represent good value and the opportunity to see some less-visited ports as ships migrate from one cruising area to another. One such example is the fleet that moves from Alaska to the Caribbean via the Panama Canal. The Canary Islands are a popular winter destination for cruises, as are Hawaii, the South Pacific and the Far East.

If you are extremely prone to motion sickness, a river cruise or a cruise in a sheltered coastal area may be a good introduction to cruising. Alaska loop cruises along the Inside Passage, for example, are usually very smooth.

Once you have determined your travel budget, destination of choice, time of year and length of vacation, the next question is, 'Which cruise line?' Although most cruise passengers spend a great deal of time on shore exploring each port of call, the ship itself is an important part of the vacation. On a typical 10-day Caribbean cruise, for example, three full days are spent at sea, so it's important to choose a ship with an atmosphere you enjoy. Your travel agent will be able to help you here, as will this book with its description of the various cruise lines in Chapter 5.

One approach is to consider the type of vacation you want, i.e. one that is active, restful, adventurous, cultural or educational? If you want lots of physical activity and excitement, a cruise line that attracts a young, energetic crowd may be what you want. If you have children, choose a cruise line with youth facilities and supervised activities for various age groups. Do note, however, that some cruise lines do not accept children under six months of age and, although children's programs are free, there is usually an hourly charge for babysitting services. If you are looking forward to peace and quiet, or perhaps a romantic interlude, then ask about cruise lines with a refined atmosphere where you can unwind at your leisure.

Generally speaking, the budget and popular-priced lines attract a younger crowd than do the premium and luxury lines. A few, such as Dolphin and Premier, cater specifically to families with children, but most of the popular-priced lines have good facilities and supervised activities for young passengers. Even the premium lines, while generally attracting an older clientele, offer programs for children during school vacations. Also, most modern cruise ships contain both adjoining cabins and ones that can accommodate families. Sun-and-sand destinations are more popular with young cruisers than sightseeing-oriented regions such as Alaska and Europe. The fares charged to children, from infancy to age eighteen, vary considerably from line to line.

Ships that offer a more relaxed and refined cruise atmosphere tend to be the luxury and premium ships. Bigger does not always mean better, and some of the highest rated ships in the world are small but very spacious, such as those of Seabourn Cruise Line and Cunard's *Sea Goddess I & II*. These luxury-priced small ships focus on providing a personalized cruise of exquisite service and interesting port itineraries. The premium-priced lines appeal to couples seeking a pampered vacation and an array of adult activities.

Some ships, especially the new megaships, have such a wide range of accommodations, facilities and activities, they appeal to all types of passengers. On the other hand, specialty 'destination' cruise lines appeal to a narrower market with their expedition-like approach and focus on learning. River cruises, in Europe especially, also have an academic ambiance and are culturally enlightening.

When deciding on a specific ship, be aware that the newer ships (those built in the late '80s and '90s) tend to be more spacious than earlier ships. They contain an abundance of public areas and their cabins are fairly roomy, with a limited number specifically designed for passengers with wheelchairs. Older ships have smaller windows or portholes and less public area, but they often have loyal followings due to their traditional charm and an intimacy new ships sometimes lack. These classic liners also have more single cabins than do contemporary ships, and most lines charge solo passengers a hefty single supplement when occupying a double cabin. Single supplements vary from line to line, so a knowledgeable travel agent should be consulted in this regard.

AT A GLANCE – CRUISE LINE CATEGORIES

The following is a list of the major lines serving North American cruise vacationers and a sampling of their ships. (Sister ships not listed would be in same category as one shown.)

Luxury-Priced

Crystal Cruises: *Crystal Harmony*
Cunard: *QE2, Royal Viking Sun, Sagafjord, Sea Goddess I & II*
Radisson Seven Seas Cruises: *Radisson Diamond, Songof Flower, Hanseatic*
Seabourn Cruise Line: *Seabourn Pride*
Silversea Cruises: *Silver Cloud*
Windstar Cruises: *Wind Song*

Premium-Priced

Celebrity Cruises: *Century, Zenith, Meridian*
Costa Cruise Lines: *Costa Romantica*
Cunard: *Crown Dynasty*
Holland America Line: *Statendam, Nieuw Amsterdam, Westerdam, Rotterdam*
Majesty Cruise Line: *Royal Majesty*
Norwegian Cruise Line: *Norway*
P&O: *Oriana, Victoria*
Princess Cruises: *Royal Princess, Sun Princess*
Renaissance Cruises: *Renaissance I to VIII*
Royal Caribbean Cruise Line: *Legend of the Seas, Sovereign of the Seas, Song of America*

Popular-Priced

American Hawaii Cruises: *Constitution,*
Carnival Cruise Lines: *Tropicale, Jubilee, Ecstasy, Imagination*
Costa Cruise Lines: *Costa Marina, Costa Allegra*
Norwegian Cruise Line: *Leeward, Windward*
Premier Cruise Lines: *Star/Ship Atlantic, Star/Ship Oceanic*
Princess Cruises: *Regal Princess, Star Princess*
Royal Caribbean Cruise Line: *Sun Viking, Song of Norway*

Budget–Priced

Dolphin Cruise Line: *Dolphin IV, Ocean Breeze*
P&O: *Canberra*

Expedition

> **Alaska Sightseeing Cruise West**: *Spirit of Alaska,*
> *Spirit of '98*
> **Orient Lines:** *Marco Polo*
> **P&O:** *Spice Islander, Island Explorer*
> **World Explorer Cruises:** *Enchanted Seas*

YOUR CABIN

For passengers who plan to spend most of their time enjoying the ship's public facilities, a cabin's size and amenities are of little consequence. For those who plan frequent retreats to their quarters, a larger cabin may be a priority. It's important to be clear about this when booking your cruise because, once on board, it can be difficult or impossible to change accommodations. Ships are often fully booked and the highest grade cabins are usually occupied, leaving little selection for passengers disgruntled with their accommodation.

Make sure your travel agent fully understands your expectations regarding accommodation. Your agent should explain to you exactly what you are getting terms of cabin space – from size and bed arrangement to

Standard cabins on cruise ships can vary in size but most are efficient and comfortable and usually include twin beds that can be converted to a double. Shown here is an outside stateroom on P&O's Oriana.

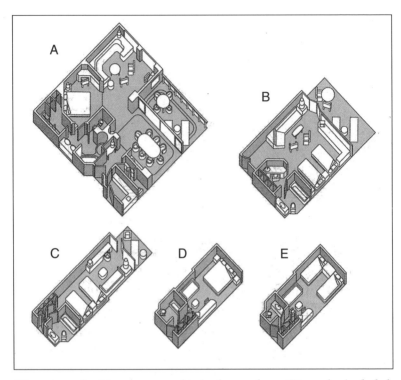

The range of cabins on a new ship is shown above. (Verandas included in measurements.) A – Penthouse Suite; 1,126 sq. ft. B – Deluxe Suite with veranda; 600 sq. ft. C – Stateroom with veranda; 284 sq. ft. D – Outside cabin; 196 sq. ft. E – Inside cabin; 186 sq. ft.

bathroom facilities. Remember too that everyone on board enjoys the same meals, entertainment and access to public facilities regardless of their private acommodation.

Each cruise line brochure contains diagrams of the ship's decks, with all cabins numbered and coded according to their grade. Careful perusal of these diagrams will reveal the location of each cabin. When deciding where on the ship you would like to sleep, there are a number of factors to consider. If the ship's motion is a concern, choose a cabin in the middle part of the ship. Cabins located near the aft end of the ship are subject to more engine vibration than those located forward. Passengers in cabins located far forward will experience the most motion if the ship's bow is plowing through a heavy sea. If you are a light sleeper and don't like noise, ensure your cabin is away from the discos or casino. If you have young children, you may want to locate yourself close to the ship's play-room. And passengers with physical handicaps should try to position themselves near the elevators rather than at the far end of a long corridor. (Passengers with wheelchairs choose from those cabins specifically designed for their special needs. On the newer ships, there is a larger selection of such cabins.)

The higher decks usually contain the largest and most expensive cabins, located outside and sometimes featuring verandas. The next deck down will have lower grades of cabins – usually smaller and with fewer facilities, such as a shower instead of a bath, a window instead of a veranda. The lower passenger decks will contain the least-expensive grades of cabins. Some of these will be located inside with no window or porthole, and may contain a bed that converts into a couch for daytime use. A cabin located on the boat deck may have its view partially blocked by a lifeboat, and those on the promenade deck will have people walking past but the window's one-way glass preserves the occupants' privacy.

When booking your accommodation, you can reserve a specific cabin (assuming it's still available for a particular cruise) or you can book a level of cabin at a guaranteed rate with the possibility that you may be upgraded. A cruise line will upgrade you to a more expensive cabin if it subsequently receives bookings in excess of the cabins available at the lower price level. Many people take advantage of these free upgrades by

Large outside cabins include a sitting area in addition to two twin beds (or a large single bed). Shown above is an outside stateroom with veranda on Norwegian Cruise Line's Windward.

booking well in advance at a guaranteed rate. Others prefer to know exactly where on the ship their cabin is located and feel this is more important than being moved into a larger cabin that might not be ideally situated according to their personal preferences.

Booking Your Cruise

People who plan their vacation well in advance can take advantage of the cruise lines' early booking discounts. These can be significant and the earlier you book, the deeper the discount. Other advantages to booking early include the wide choice of cabins available and the opportunity for potential upgrades. A reduced fare can also be obtained if you are making a group booking. Couples or foursomes traveling together can save money by booking a 'quad' cabin instead of two double cabins – assuming everyone in the party is compatible! And last but not least, you can wait for last-minute cabin sales. Base ports, such as Miami and Fort Lauderdale for the Caribbean and Vancouver for Alaska, are occasionally used as a 'dumping ground' for these sales which are good value for people who live in the vicinity and are able to hop on a ship at short notice.

In recent years an expanding list of new ships has entered the cruise market and the fares being offered have become increasingly competitive. When there are more berths available than passengers filling them, the market is said to be in a state of over capacity and this has prompted the cruise companies to discount their fares in an effort to fill all their cabins. The Caribbean, which is serviced by the highest number of ships, is one region where discounts have become commonplace. Other areas, such as Alaska, usually sell out during the peak summer months. There are, however, early booking discounts offered for any cruising area. So, regardless of the area you wish to cruise, an early booking will usually get you the best deal. Some cruise lines protect those booking early with a guarantee against future discounts – to ensure the early bird truly gets the best berth.

Most cruise lines require a deposit to confirm your reservation, with the balance due about 60 days prior to your departure date. If you are making a last-minute booking, the entire fare must be paid in full. Payment of your cruise fare can be made with a credit card or cheque. In the unlikely event of a cruise line shutting down operations, the consumer is protected by federal maritime law and will either be reimbursed or provided with an alternative cruise of comparable value in a similar time frame.

Should you wish to cancel your booking after the balance has been paid in full, the amount refunded depends on the individual cruise line's policy and when your notice of cancellation is received. To receive a full refund, most lines insist on notification at least 60 days prior to sailing, with some requiring up to 90 days. Should you wish to cancel after a certain date, a cancellation charge is deducted from your refund. For example, if you cancel six weeks prior to sailing, the cruise company's cancellation charge might be anywhere from 20% to 50% of the total fare; if you cancel 15 days prior to sailing, the charge could be as much as 75%; and should you fail to embark on the cruise, you will probably have to forfeit 100% of your cruise fare. Each cruise line has its own cancellation policy and its details are explained in fine type under 'General Information' near the back of the brochure. You should read these pages carefully. Port taxes are sometimes additional and these vary from about $50 to $200 per passenger depending on the length of cruise and its itinerary.

Cruise lines recommend buying cancellation insurance, which protects you in the event that unforeseeable circumstances prevent you from taking your cruise. The cost, generally under $100 for a 7-day cruise, is money well spent.

If you plan to book an all-inclusive vacation package through the cruise line, arrangements for air flights, hotel accommodations, and pre- or post-land tours must all be made when you book your cruise. Optional shore excursions at the ports of call can be booked once you are on the cruise.

When making your cruise booking, be sure to indicate your preferred sitting for dinner (first or second), the size of table at which you would like to dine (i.e. table for two, four, six or eight), whether you prefer a smoking or non-smoking section, and any special dietary requirements you may have (i.e. diabetic, kosher or vegetarian). If you are bringing a young child on board and need a crib, this should be requested at the time of booking.

The ability of a cruise line to accommodate your special requests can be verified by your travel agent prior to booking.

CRUISE SELECTOR

The following check list may help you narrow down your vacation preferences and assist your travel agent in directing you toward the appropriate cruise line and ship.

Major Destinations: ✓

Alaska	
Asia/Pacific	
Bermuda	
Canary Islands/North Africa	
Caribbean/Bahamas/Florida	
Europe/Baltic	
Hawaii	
Mediterranean	
Mexican Riviera	
New England/Eastern Canada	
Panama Canal	
Scandinavia	
Transatlantic	

Expedition/River Destinations: ✓

Amazon	
Antarctica	
Arctic	
European Waterways	
Far East Rivers	
Galapagos	
Nile	
North American Rivers	

Travel Budget *(per person, not including children who cruise for less, depending on age and cruise line)* ✓

Under $1,000	
$1,000 to $2,000	
$2,000 to $4,000	
$4,000 to $6,000	
$6,000 to $10,000	
$10,000+	

C R U I S E   S E L E C T O R

	✓
Time of Year	✓
Winter	
Spring	
Summer	
Fall	
Type of Cruise Line **(Cost/Passenger Market/ Atmosphere)**	✓
Budget-Priced/Families/Casual	
Popular-Priced/All Age Groups/Casual	
Popular-to-Premium Priced/All Age Groups/Semi–Formal	
Premium-Priced/Mature Passengers/Semi–formal	
Luxury-Priced/Affluent Adults/Formal	
Size of Ship	✓
Classic Liner	
Modern Cruise Liner	
Megaship	
Luxury Small Ship	
Specialty Cruises	✓
River Cruises	
Sailing Ships	
Expedition	
Length of Cruise	✓
3 to 4 nights	
4 nights to 1 week	
1 to 2 weeks	
2 weeks to 1 month	
1 to 3 months	
Type of Cabin	✓
Basic Inside	
Outside	
Outside with Veranda	
Mini-suite	
Suite	
Single	

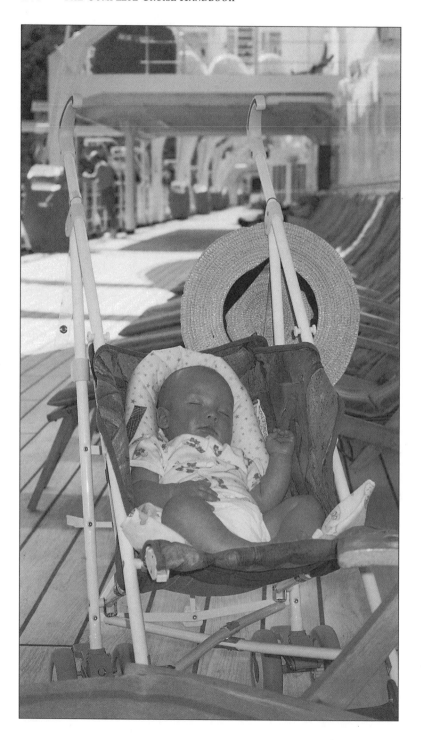

CHAPTER SEVEN

PREPARING FOR YOUR CRUISE

T he wonderful thing about preparing for a cruise is the lack of effort required. Once you are on board the ship, the captain and crew will handle all travel concerns and your time will be your own to do with as you please. So, to ensure you make the best use of your holiday time, this chapter will address some of the questions you may have about preparing for a cruise.

Documentation

Passports & Visas

Identification requirements vary throughout the world, which is why a valid passport is the best proof of citizenship a traveler can carry. American and Canadian citizens are not required to carry a passport when visiting each other's countries or those of the Caribbean, including Mexico. However, you are required to carry a birth certificate or a certified copy of one, accompanied by an official photo identification such as a driver's license. For American travelers, a U.S. naturalization certificate, accompanied by an official photo identification, is also acceptable. All non-U.S. and non-Canadian citizens must carry a valid passport and any necessary visas or, in the case of a U.S. resident alien, an Alien Registration Receipt Card. Your travel agent can advise if a passport and any visas are required for the ports of call included in your cruise.

Travel Documents

A few weeks before your departure date (and upon payment in full of your cruise fare), the cruise line will send you all pertinent documentation which usually includes your cruise ticket, airline ticket (if applicable), luggage tags, a customs and immigration form, and information on shore tours and other aspects of the cruise, often in booklet form. All of this documentation should be read carefully and a detailed itinerary left behind with a family member, friend and/or neighbor in case someone back home needs to contact you while you're away. Be sure to include the name of your ship, its phone number and the applicable ocean code, as well as your cabin number – all of which will be included in your cruise documents. With this information, a person can call the international telephone operator and place a satellite call to your ship in an emergency.

Another precaution you should take before leaving home is to photocopy on a single sheet of paper the identification page of your passport (with photo and passport number on it), your drivers licence and any credit cards you will be carrying in your wallet. Keep one copy of this sheet with you, separate from your passport and wallet, and leave another one at home.

Insurance

Most travel agents recommend a travel insurance policy at the time of booking. A comprehensive policy will cover trip cancellation, delayed departure, medical expenses, personal accident and liability, lost baggage and money, and legal expenses.

You may already have supplementary health insurance through a credit card, automobile club policy or employment health plan, but you should check these carefully. Whatever policy you choose for your trip, carry details of it with you and documents showing that you are covered by a plan. You and your travelling companions should know how to contact your insurer, as should your travel agent and someone at home.

If you need medical attention while away, obtain a detailed invoice from the doctor or hospital for submission to the insurance company upon your return. Passengers who use wheelchairs or prosthetic devices should be sure these are included in any personal effects insurance they purchase. Pregnant women should check that complications arising from their condition are also covered. (Note: Most cruise lines will not accept female passengers who are in their third trimester of pregnancy.)

Health Precautions

Vaccinations and Medical Attention

Vaccinations are rarely compulsory for holidays featured in cruise brochures, however immunization against various infectious diseases is recommended for certain parts of the world. Consult your doctor for advice in this regard.

In some less developed countries it's prudent to avoid drinking the water and buying food from street vendors. If you have a concern, question your shore excursion manager. Bottled water can usually be bought on the ship for taking ashore.

All large ships have a fully equipped medical center with a doctor and nurses. Passengers needing medical attention are billed at private rates which are added to their shipboard account. This invoice can be submitted to your insurance company upon your return home.

Seasickness

Although motion sickness is not a widespread or prolonged problem with most passengers, there are a number of remedies for those susceptible to this affliction. One is to wear special wrist bands, the balls of which rest on an acupressure point. These 'sea bands' are available in most drugstores. Another option is to chew Meclizine tablets (often available at the ship's front office) or take Dramamine pills. It's best to take these pills ahead of time, before you feel too nauseous, and they may make you drowsy. A third solution is to wear a Scolpolamine patch behind one ear, but these are known to produce side effects such as dizziness and blurred vision. Check first with your doctor before deciding on any medication.

Fresh air is one of the best antidotes to motion sickness, so stepping out on deck is often all that's needed to counter any queeziness. Other simple remedies include sipping on ginger ale and nibbling on dry crackers and an apple. Lying down also helps. Should you become concerned about your condition, visit the medical center on board for professional attention.

What to Pack

Clothing

If you are embarking on a fly/cruise, you will be limited by the airline to two suitcases and one carry-on bag per person. This same restriction usually applies to cruise passengers taking a land tour before or after their cruise. Some cruise lines have their own baggage restrictions which are outlined in the 'General Information' section at the back of each brochure. People tend to travel lighter these days and, with a bit of planning, everything you need for a one-to two-week cruise can fit into one or two suitcases.

Pack casual attire for daytime wear – both on board the ship and in port. The best approach is to dress in layers, especially in cooler climates, rather than pack bulky sweaters and coats. Mixing and matching is another key to stretching a travel wardrobe, as is the use of accessories –

scarves, jewelry, belts – that can be used to dress a basic outfit up or down, depending on the dress code in the dining room that evening.

For formal evenings on board the ship, women wear gowns or cocktail dresses and men favor black tie or dark suits. For informal evenings, women wear dresses, skirts or slacks, while men wear jackets with either a shirt and tie or an open-necked sports shirt. Contrary to what many women expect, a cruise is not an on-going fashion parade among the passengers. On the premium and popular-priced cruises, most people dress modestly, apart from the few formal evenings when everyone seems to enjoy the opportunity to dress in their finest.

Footwear is also important. Your shoes and sandals should be comfortable, preferably with rubber soles to prevent slipping on the ship's decks, and leather uppers are preferable to canvas should they get wet. You may want to pack one pair of shoes for walking about on shore (where they may get dirty) and another for strolling about the ship. Give your shore shoes a good spray of all-weather protector before packing them. Headgear is another consideration. A wide-brimmed hat is recommended – one made of straw for the tropics and of felt for cooler cruising areas.

Most ships have launderettes which are either free or coin-operated, with soap automatically dispensed into the washer. An iron and ironing board are usually installed in each launderette. Passengers can also have their laundry done for them, as well as steam pressing and dry cleaning, all at an additional expense which is added to your shipboard account.

Other Items

You may want to pack a small pair of binoculars for viewing the sights from the ship's deck. This is especially applicable on cruises that feature frequent sightings of marine life such as Alaska, and on river cruises. Sunglasses are also recommended because of glare off the water, even on cloudy days.

Keep any prescribed medication in original, labeled containers and carry a doctor's prescription for any controlled drug. If you wear prescription eyeglasses or contact lenses, consider packing a spare pair. And keep all valuables (travelers cheques, camera, expensive jewelry) in your carry-on luggage, as well as all prescription medicines and documentation (passport, tickets, insurance policy).

The shops on board the large ships contain toiletries for passengers who forget to pack an essential item. They also feature luxury goods – designer clothes, perfumes, jewelry, gifts and souvenirs – at duty-free prices. Other products sold on board include film and duty-free liquor.

If you're bringing a baby, pack plenty of diapers in case the ship has a limited supply. Children will want to bring a few toys and games to play with in their cabin. And everyone should leave some room in their suitcases for souvenirs.

Reading Material

For passengers who didn't pack their own reading material, the ship's library will have magazines, paperbacks and books on a variety of subjects, both fiction and non-fiction. However, the librarian may not let you check out any guidebooks on the area you are cruising, so that all passengers have access to their information, and you may want to purchase beforehand an informative guidebook about the ports of call you will be visiting. Most cruise lines do provide some helpful port information either in the daily program (slipped under you cabin door each day) or on a separate print-out that is often available at the Front Desk or Shore Excursion Office. There may also be a magazine in your cabin with information about the destinations you will be visiting in the course of your cruise.

Joining Your Cruise

This detail will be handled when you book your cruise, as most cruise lines offer special fares on flights and coach transfers to the ship's pier. Often a cruise line representative is on hand at the port city's airport to direct passengers to a waiting coach that will take them to the ship.

Once you reach the ship terminal, there will be cruise line representatives milling about to help passengers with any questions they might have. Passengers are processed quickly and efficiently once the ship is ready for embarkation and there's plenty of time for everyone to board. In fact, after the initial rush, most passengers do not have to wait.

Most cruise lines allow a few hours for embarkation. For instance, a ship leaving port at 5:00 p.m. will usually start boarding at about 2:00 p.m. (sometimes earlier) and no later than 3:00 p.m. Passengers are usually asked to be on board no later than a half-hour prior to its sailing time.

Should you decide to make your own travel arrangements and these involve an air flight, you may want to arrive at the port of embarkation the day before your cruise commences and avoid the nail-biting prospect of arriving too late to catch the ship should your flight be delayed. If you have booked an all-inclusive package with the cruise line, the time logistics will have been worked out for you. Nonetheless, you may still prefer to arrive in port the day before your cruise begins so that you are rested and relaxed the moment you step on board the ship instead of feeling tired from a full day of making travel connections.

Boarding the Ship

When you arrive at the cruise terminal, your luggage (apart from carry-on bags) is handled by the longshoremen. You will have been provided with identification tags by the cruise line (part of your cruise ticket documentation) which must be attached to each piece of luggage. This tag identifies the ship on which you are sailing and contains your name and cabin number. Shortly after boarding, your luggage will be brought to your stateroom by your cabin steward or stewardess. He or she will be looking after your cabin and any requests you may have for the duration of the cruise.

A ship hums with activity just prior to sailing as passengers and their luggage are brought on board. Bon voyage celebrations often take place in the cabin if its occupants are lucky enough to have a chilled bottle of bubbly awaiting them. Some passengers, after locating their cabins, prefer to wander the decks and explore the ship. It should be noted that, with security a high priority, most cruise lines no longer allow visitors on board the ships prior to departure.

ON BOARD
Your Cabin

Unless you have booked a suite, your cabin will be smaller than a standard hotel room. It will, however, be kept spotless by your cabin steward.

Twice a day your cabin will be cleaned – once in the morning while you're at breakfast or ashore at a port of call, and again in the evening while you're at dinner. In cabins containing a couch that converts into a bed, this will be taken care of by your cabin steward who will turn your bed down each evening and make it up every morning. Twice daily soiled towels will be replaced, wastepaper baskets emptied and the bathroom cleaned.

Storage space is limited but a basic cabin will contain a closet for hanging dresses and suits, and drawers to hold other clothes. Basic toiletries, such as soap, shampoo and hand lotion, are usually provided, and a hair dryer may or may not be installed in the bathroom, something you can determine at the time of booking.

Beach towels for taking ashore will be provided by your steward on request, and deck towels can be found near the swimming pool. Any special requests, such as having your clothes laundered or dry cleaned, are handled by your cabin steward.

Dinner Reservations

Breakfast and lunch on board a cruise ship are usually open seating, with meals served between set times. For dinner, however, you will be assigned a specific table at which the same waiter will serve you each evening. If you've booked onto a luxury ship, it will probably have only one sitting at dinner and often with open seating.

When booking your cruise, you will be asked to indicate your preference for the first or second sitting at dinner, the size of table at which you would like to sit, and whether you want to be in a smoking or non-smoking section of the dining room. The earlier you book a cruise, the better your chance of being assigned your preferences.

Upon embarkation, you will find a note in your cabin confirming your table number and whether it's for the first or second sitting. If you want to change this, you should promptly visit the front office and submit your request which the maitre d'hotel will try to accommodate but cannot guarantee.

Some people prefer the first sitting because it gives them an entire evening afterwards to enjoy the stage show or other entertainment on board the ship. And if your appetite has returned by the end of the evening, you can stop by the midnight buffet. Early risers also tend to favor the first sitting.

On the other hand, the second sitting allows passengers plenty of time, after a full day in port, to freshen up and relax before dinner. Ships often depart a port at about five o'clock in the afternoon and passengers who choose the late sitting can linger on deck as the ship sails away and, if cruising in the tropics, they can enjoy the sunset before retiring to their cabins to change for dinner.

The Ship's Staff

In the course of your cruise, you will come to recognize some of the ship's staff – especially those with high-profile positions such as the cruise director, who is in charge of entertainment on board the ship. Passengers interested in booking shore excursions will get to know the shore excursion manager, and of course your cabin steward and dining room steward are two people you will see on a daily basis. In charge of the large hotel staff is the ship's hotel manager (sometimes called the chief purser) whose responsibility it is to make sure every passenger is happy with the service they are receiving.

Separate from the hotel staff are the captain, chief engineer, and their officers and crew, who are responsible for the safe and efficient running of the ship. The captain is ultimately in charge of the entire ship and his role includes not only overseeing the officers on the bridge but fulfilling a social role on behalf of the cruise line. The captain and the hotel manager greet every passenger who attends the captain's welcome aboard cocktail party, usually held the second night of a cruise, and he will occasionally dine with selected passengers at the captain's table.

Passengers with inquiries or seeking assistance can visit the Front Office (also called the Purser's Office) where their needs will be handled by the appropriate staff member.

The Front Office on a cruise ship handles all passenger inquiries and is where your shipboard account is settled. The hotel manager is in charge of ensuring passenger satisfaction.

Lifeboat Drill

A mandatory safety drill involving all passengers is carried out on all ships within 24 hours of its departure. Many of the cruise lines conduct this drill before the ship even pulls away from the dock. Passengers are instructed over the loudspeaker system to don their lifejackets, which are stored in their cabin, and proceed to their appointed lifeboat station. Instructions are usually posted on the inside of the cabin door and your steward is always nearby to lend assistance.

Once all the ship's passengers have congregated on the boat deck at their designated stations (these are numbered), a member of the ship's crew will check off each passenger's name to make sure everyone is in attendance. A demonstration then follows showing how the lifeboats will be lowered into the water in the unlikely event of an abandon-ship emergency. Once this procedure is finished – and the entire drill takes about 20 minutes – passengers may return to their cabins, remove their lifejackets and stow them in their proper place. It's now time for everyone to completely relax and do whatever they desire which, for most people, is standing at the rail and waving to bystanders on shore as the ship eases away from the dock and the cruise begins.

Shipboard Account

Most ships are cashless societies in which passengers simply sign for incidental expenses such as drinks in a bar, dry cleaning, massages, facials and haircuts. Even purchases in the on-board shops are signed to your cabin. At the end of the cruise, an itemized statement of account will be delivered to your cabin. This account can, on most cruise lines, be settled by credit card, personal cheque or cash. You can confirm this beforehand either by reading the fine print at the back of the cruise brochure or perusing the packet of information that arrives with your cruise ticket.

Tipping

Although tipping is a cruising tradition, no passenger is obligated to hand out tips at the end of a cruise. However, most passengers respond to the service they receive and enjoy rewarding the people who have served them. Your cruise line will no doubt provide you with guidelines on how much to tip various staff, but a general rule is to tip your cabin steward about $3.00 per passenger per day, your waiter the same amount, and your busboy half that amount. Your wine steward should receive 10 to 15 percent of your total wine bill, although some cruise lines include gratuities for bar staff and wine waiters in all beverage bills. Some of the luxury ships have a no-tipping policy. Tips are usually given the last night of the cruise, in envelopes provided.

Going Ashore

At each port of call the ship will either dock or anchor. Most cruise lines are willing to pay the dock fees rather than anchor, which entails lowering the tenders (small boats) for transporting passengers ashore. Generally speaking, ships anchor when there is no dock space left or proper dock facilities do not exist at a particular port. Dock space is reserved in advance by each cruise line and it's possible to find out, either by reading the cruise brochure or asking your travel agent, at which ports the ship will be docking versus anchoring.

When your ship pulls into a port at which it drops anchor, there will be a minor delay in getting ashore. Passengers who have booked soon-to-begin shore excursions are transported ashore first, followed by those who have proceeded to a designated area to obtain a number for boarding a tender. However, because the ships usually pull into port early in the morning, most people don't even notice the delay because they're often still in the dining room having breakfast or in their cabins enjoying a leisurely start to the day when the tenders start heading ashore. By the time many of the passengers are ready to go ashore, there is no longer any wait involved.

At some ports of call the ship will anchor and passengers are taken ashore in the ship's tenders. Shown here is a tender heading ashore at Haines, Alaska.

Getting back to the ship is simply a matter of returning to the dock at which you disembarked from the tender. A ship's officer is stationed there throughout the day, supervising the coming and going of tenders. You can catch a ride back to the ship at any time during the ship's stay in port and, although lineups tend to form in the last hour prior to the ship's departure, these move quickly.

For tardy passengers who return to the tender dock in time to see their ship raising anchor and steaming away from port, a dock worker may be able to radio the ship. The officer on the bridge will either lower a tender to retrieve the stranded passengers or a pilot boat might be engaged to whisk the latecomers out to the ship while it waits. The only penalty for such tardiness is extreme embarassment as people watch from the rail while these wayward passengers are brought on board and the ship can finally get underway. Anyone who fails to return to the ship after it has left port, however, is responsible for costs incurred in getting to the next port of call to reconnect with the cruise.

Shopping

Cruise vacationers look forward to shopping at each port of call, especially where items can be purchased at bargain prices. Time is of the essence when in port, so try to research the cost of luxury items before you leave home. Many of the cruise lines hire on-board consultants who recommend specific items and specific shops at each port of call. These recommended merchants often pay a promotional fee to the cruise line; in return, the line's passengers are guaranteed of the integrity of goods they purchase and can usually turn to the cruise line for assistance should a dispute arise concerning merchandise.

Duty-free goods have had no import tax added to their price, while goods purchased in their country of manufacture are duty exempt, which is why locally handcrafted items are often well worth purchasing. Loose gems such as rubies, emeralds, diamonds and sapphires are also duty exempt.

The Caribbean is well known for its port shopping, where most islands impose a low import duty and no sales tax. Many ports offer substantial savings on leather, linen, liquor, jewelry, watches, perfumes, cameras and electronics. The United States Virgin Islands are the most popular with American visitors who enjoy generous duty-free allowances when shopping there.

When heading ashore at any port, always take some small bills to pay for miscellaneous items such as postcards or cab fare. Travelers cheques can be cashed on board the ship.

Before you embark on your cruise, you may want to visit your local

Each port of call presents the opportunity to shop for locally-made goods which are duty exempt.

customs office and register any valuables you plan to take with you (i.e. cameras, jewelry) so that you have no problem reimporting them duty and tax free.

Phoning Home

Passengers wishing to place a ship-to-shore telephone call need only contact the ship's radio office and request that either a satellite or radio call be placed. Satellite telephone calls are the most convenient option, providing a high-quality connection and complete privacy. On newer ships these calls can be dialed directly on your cabin telephone or at phones installed in various public areas around the ship. The only drawback to placing such a call is the expense – about $8 per minute. Radio calls are less expensive than satellite calls but are not private, can be time consuming to place, and may fade in and out.

If the call is not urgent, you may want to wait and place it from a land-based phone at the next port of call. The pre-paid telephone calling card, a new telecommunications product, is an easy way for passengers to place long-distance calls while in port. Sold on board some ships, these cards allow the user to make international and domestic calls from any touchtone phone.

Holiday Photos

A pleasant aspect of cruise travel is the presence of professional photographers on board the ship. They are there to capture highlights of each passenger's cruise experience such as embarkation, the captain's welcome aboard cocktail party, and formal nights in the dining room. The ship's photographers also mingle with passengers throughout the days and evenings, capturing happy and impromptu moments on film. All of their prints are displayed in the ship's photo gallery where passengers can view them at their leisure and order any they may want to keep.

Of course, many travelers are keen to take their own photographs, especially at the various ports of call. The serious camera buff will need no advice but point-and-shoot photographers may benefit from a few tips. First, if you are taking a brand-new camera on your trip, shoot and develop a roll of film at home to make sure the camera works properly and that you understand all its features. Second, pack more film than you anticipate using rather than waste holiday time looking for shops that sell fresh film at reasonable prices. For automatic cameras, 200-ASA print film is your best choice for all-around lighting conditions. Make sure you've got fresh batteries in the camera and remember to have fun with your picture taking. Be spontaneous and creative rather than analytical when framing a shot. The subject matter should fill the frame so move in closer if there's a lot of superfluous space in your viewfinder.

Disembarkation

On the final night of the cruise you will likely be asked to leave your packed and tagged suitcases outside your cabin door before retiring for the night. This is standard procedure if disembarkation is taking place the next morning. Keep all valuables and travel documents with you in your carry-on bag, as well as the outfit you plan to wear the next day. Many a cruise director has a story to tell about passengers who pack all of their clothes before going to bed and realize the next morning that they have only their pyjamas to wear off the ship!

Assuming you have kept clothes to wear the last morning of your cruise, you can usually enjoy a leisurely albeit early breakfast before disembarkation announcements begin over the PA system. Most large ships disembark passengers in groups – those with early flights to catch are disembarked first – and the last batch of passengers is usually off the ship by mid-morning.

Your luggage will be waiting for you in the cruise terminal where you pick it up before proceeding through Customs & Immigration (if returning home) or boarding a coach for transfer to the airport and your flight home.

CHAPTER EIGHT

NEW SHIPS – NEW HORIZONS

The '90s have been one of busiest decades this century for passenger ship building. Some of the largest ships ever built are being launched and they keep getting bigger, with ships over 100,000 tons just around the corner.

This rapid pace of ship construction is expected to continue almost to the end of the decade, with over 20 new ships either contracted or planned for construction. And this is good news for vacationers planning a cruise because it means greater diversity in ship selection, an expanding list of itineraries, and competitive fares as cruise lines vie for passengers and market share.

The ship of the future has already been revealed in some recent launches. Ships are being built higher, especially in the stern area, to provide greater interior space, and most new ships have cabins located more forward and aft than even a few years ago. As a result, new ships receive the deserved complaint that they are box-like in appearance. On the plus side, these new ships are providing a higher percentage of outside cabins – especially ones with verandas – and cabins are generally becoming more spacious. Overall, the trend is to provide more boat for the buck. Public areas such as lounges, restaurants, theaters and viewing areas are all becoming larger. And since these areas are open to all, every passenger, no matter what level of cabin, benefits.

Naval architects have acknowledged that ships will probably not get much larger than 100,000 tons (or 3,000-passenger capacity). The reason is a sharp decline in efficiency of design beyond this size – the ship ends up with too much interior space which would have to be filled with inside cabins (something many passengers don't want) or with low-revenue-pro-ducing public areas (something the cruise lines don't want).

One important improvement in design is in the ecology of new ships. The 'green' theme is now an accepted principle and this is why cruise ships are rarely cited as a contributor to pollution. All sewage is processed on board, the ships usually burn high-grade fuel with low emissions, and all garbage is either processed on board or compressed for recycling at an appropriate port. A new 'green' ship might deposit as little as one dump-ster of garbage at the end of a seven-day cruise.

A growing trend in ship construction is the building of sister ships, with some cruise lines ordering three or four at a time. This allows the ship builder to take advantage of some assembly-line efficiencies and save money. The sister ship concept also helps the cruise lines hone their product so that their quality of service is maintained from ship to ship. Experienced staff on one ship can move to a sister ship without losing stride.

Passenger needs are the main factor in new ship construction. With pas-sengers now taking a more holistic approach to their vacations, combining exercise with fine dining and fun with learning, naval architects have responded to this with ships offering a wide selection of facilities and varied public areas. Cramped poolsides are out, elegance and space are in.

Today's diverse marketplace has prompted the cruise companies to better define themselves to potential customers. Each line has its own approach to the motif and finished quality of the ship's interior, designed to establish a certain atmosphere. Holland America Line, for example, uses its Dutch naval tradition as a theme throughout the fleet.

Distinguishing design elements are also incorporated on a ship's exte-rior to set one fleet apart from another. Carnival Cruise Lines' hallmark is the winged funnel on each of its ships; Celebrity ships are instantly recog-nizable by the large X painted on the funnel; and Royal Caribbean Cruise Line's ships have a distinct profile with a circular lounge wrapped around the funnel.

Engineering advances in construction of new ships are stunning. Ships of 50,000 tons that used to take four years to build now take less than a year. Ships used to be built by cutting steel from full sized wooden tem-plates – now all calculations and cutting are done by computer. And, by welding prefabricated sections of the ship together, instead of riveting individual plates as in the past, the hull of the ship is lighter and stronger.

The diesel engines on new ships are rubber mounted and almost vibra-tion-free. This has allowed large open dining rooms or show lounges to be positioned at the stern of the ship where the width gives plenty of space and guests won't be rattling around in their seats. Insulation has also greatly improved, making for the age of the 'quiet' ship.

The introduction of the glass-domed atrium on large cruise ships creates the pleasant effect of bringing light deep into the central part of the ship and also serves as a point of reference, making it easier for passengers to orient themselves with what at first seems like an immense resort. This architectural center-piece on some new ships is breath-taking. Royal Caribbean Cruise Line's *Legend of the Seas* contains a remarkable example of this design concept. The ship has a seven-deck glass-walled atrium and over two acres of glass, making for a well-lit ship with numerous vantage points for viewing the scenery. This mega-ship also features the line's trade-mark viewing lounge built around the funnel, and a two story dining room with almost no obstructions to the outside views. *Legend* also has the world's first floating 18-hole miniature golf course which has proved popular – despite the obvious water trap.

The focal point of large modern ships is the atrium, where a dramatic work of art is displayed. Shown above is the Centrum on Royal Caribbean Cruise Line's new Splendour of the Seas.

These sorts of innovations reflect the efforts of the cruise industry to provide their passengers with more choice in a range of areas such as entertainment, cuisine, recreation and family facilities. Technology has given passengers interactive television, satellite access to call home, and electronic walls depicting art, patterns or maps showing precisely where the ship is cruising. The cruise companies are well aware that in addition to being a good hotel, a ship must have a selection of activities for all age groups in order to compete with the better resorts of the world.

The efforts of cruise companies to offer greater flexibility is evident in most of this decade's newbuilds and is made possible to some extent by the fact these ships are larger and have relatively fewer people on board. Ships built in the '50s and '60s tended to accommodate more people per ton of ship. This is referred to as the space ratio and is calculated by dividing the total tonnage by the passenger capacity. This ratio began to improve over the next two decades and has accelerated in the '90s. On

A miniature golf course on the top deck of RCCL's Legend of the Seas is one of the many innovations found on today's cruise ships. Ships of the future will provide greater selection of activities for passengers.

average, a ship of this decade will have about 30% more room per passenger than a ship built in the '50s or '60s. This is a trend that appears to be here to stay.

Two major cruise lines are gearing up for the launch of new 'super-megaships' over 100,000 tons. These ships could have handled 4,000 passengers quite easily in the days when there were different classes of passengers but, in the modern era of one-class ships, they will be designed to accommodate about 2,600 passengers. For reference purposes the *Queen Elizabeth*, which until recently was the largest ship ever built (displacing 83,673 tons), had a passenger capacity of 2,300 – although during WWII it transported over 11,000 troops. Talk about lineups!

Carnival Cruise Lines' launch of *Carnival Destiny* in 1996 will introduce the largest ship ever built at what is expected to be over 100,000 tons. Constructed at a cost of over $400 million, this is a 12-deck ship with some interesting innovations. For example, most ships, even the megaships, have one large dining room. The *Destiny* will have two double-deck dining rooms with glass chandeliers and two grand staircases. And passengers who are seated in the middle of the dining room will, thanks to a raised floor, still have an ocean view.

The title of 'largest ship' may be relinquished to Princess Cruises

Carnival Destiny, 100,000+ tons, will be taller than the Statue of
Liberty and carry over 2,600 passengers. The show lounge spans three
decks and the ship has two dining rooms – each two decks high.

when it launches the *Grand Princess* in 1997. Expected to be about
104,000 tons, this ship has been loaded with an array of technological
distractions sure to keep even the most hyperactive passenger pacified.
This includes a motion-based virtual reality theater; interactive technology such as a golf driving range that will allow passengers to play on
some of the world's best-known courses; and a 'blue screen' room that
will give passengers the chance to star in their own video production so
they don't have to go to the virtual reality theater. Also, *Grand Princess*
has not one but three large show lounges, each giving passengers a different after dinner entertainment option. Perhaps the most interesting
design feature is a nightclub at the stern of the ship, suspended like a
huge wing above the other decks. This will be 15 decks above sea level
and give passengers an experience of what cruising is all about – a wonderful view of the sea and passing scenery.

While new ships are rolling off the ways, older ships will have to be
upgraded to comply with new Safety of Life at Sea (SOLAS) regulations
concerning fire prevention and evacuation. The new regulations will be
phased in starting in 1997, and the lines operating these older ships will
have to spend millions of dollars upgrading them or retire them from service. Some classic ocean liners will be history by the end of the century.

Grand Princess, at 104,000 tons, will be the world's largest cruise ship when launched in 1997. Carrying 2600 passengers the ship is too large to pass through Panama Canal.

NEW HORIZONS

Cruising has enjoyed more than a decade of phenomenal growth, and this has been a boon to many small cities and ports of the world. However, because the majority of passengers are repeat cruisers, there is a growing demand for new ports and itineraries. Some ports, especially in the Caribbean, are close to their saturation point with respect to the number of visitors they can handle, so there is an added impetus for cruise lines to find new attractions for their loyal client base. And the ports are responding.

From the east coast of Canada to the exotic Far East, ports are courting the cruise lines in an effort to be included in their new itineraries. Even the Caribbean's list of ports has expanded significantly in the last five years and cruise company executives are looking at other ports as potential new stops in the future.

One Caribbean island long overdue for the return of tourism is Cuba. Many in the industry see the cruise ships stopping here once normalization of relations with the United States occurs. Cuba, however, would require large investments in port facilities to handle the docking of big ships and the large volume of passengers, but some of this funding would probably come from the cruise companies.

The cruise lines are also looking at extending their length of stay at popular ports. Most ships remain in a port from early morning until late afternoon before steaming off to the next one. While this is adequate for some ports of call, the cruise lines have found there is a desire on the part of passengers to stay longer at certain popular destinations. Bermuda is one example of people specifically taking this cruise so they can leisurely explore the islands for three or four days while using the ship as a hotel. Some cruise lines see Barbados and the Cayman Islands as other potential 'extended time' stops meriting an extra day for passengers to completely experience the island.

Growing in popularity are short 3- and 4-day cruises, especially those out of Port Canaveral which are combined with a 3- to 4-day vacation at Walt Disney World in Orlando. Which brings us to the entry of recently-established Disney Cruise Line and the planned introduction of its first, 1,760-passenger ship – *Disney Magic* – in early 1998. A sister ship will be launched in November 1998. These are 85,000-ton megaships with lots of space set aside for children and separate attractions for adults.

Extended visits at popular destinations could also become very big in Europe. According to the World Tourism Organization, based in Madrid, land-based travel on the Continent is destined to become a lot more crowded. Tourists may have to make reservations to climb the Eiffel Tower, or book months ahead to see museums and monuments. Environmental concerns over new hotel construction are already slowing expansion of Mediterranean resorts. Over-building in prime locations is seen as compromising the original attraction of the natural scenery, making some destinations unable to cope with the growing tourist demand.

All of which continues to give cruise travel an increasing edge. Ports, in the future, may see the cruise ship as the ideal way to handle tourists and still benefit from the tourist trade. Cruise ships don't drastically alter the landscape – there is no need for large infrastructures such as hotels and parking lots. Most cruise passengers tour the local sights on foot, by shuttle bus or take a coach tour, and of course the ship is their hotel. The only thing left behind by cruise ships is the money spent by its passengers.

For the traveler of the future, cruising may be the best way to see a busy city where hotel and meal costs can be astronomical. The bustle of a city is great for a day or two but the space, comfort and relaxed pace on a ship make it a welcome retreat that cruise vacationers can look forward to at the end of a long day of sightseeing.

Most areas of the world have opened up to tourists and cruise itineraries will keep expanding to take in more and different ports, often threaded together with a common theme. Shore excursions are also evolving to meet the demands of younger cruise passengers who seek adventure and independence during their port visits.

Some cruise lines will mix a bit of adventure with an otherwise main-

Santorini, Greece

stream cruise to give passengers a unique voyage. One recent example is Crystal Cruises' 'Mysteries of the Amazon' cruise on which the ship actually journeys 700 miles up the Amazon River, stopping at ports along the way. Holland America offers a circumnavigation of South America, and another example of creative itinerary planning is the 'Solar Eclipse Cruise' that Orient Lines promoted for October of 1995 in the South China Sea.

Another welcome trend are cruises that cater to passengers who want to learn about the geography and cultures they are visiting. Mediterranean cruises with guest lecturers are especially popular for those wanting to understand the evolution of Western and Eastern cultures. Such cruises – part of the overall growth of 'theme' cruises – will impart new interest in old ports.

Perhaps of all world destinations the Far East has the most potential, simply because there are so many ports and such a diversity of cultures.

The importance of the cruise industry to this area is evident in the investment many ports have made in recent years to improve dock facilities. And it seems to be paying off – Singapore, Hong Kong, Indonesia, Malaysia, Thailand, China and even Vietnam all draw regular visits by cruise ships.

As more people see the advantage of slowing down and seeing the world from the water, more variety in cruises will be offered to the public. As the 20th century draws to a close, one of the oldest modes of transportation appears poised to become the travel holiday of the future.

GLOSSARY OF CRUISING TERMS

Aft – Near or at the **stern** (rear) of the ship.

Bow thruster – Aperture with a propeller near the front of the ship which pushes the ship sideways. Thrusters have eliminated the need for a tug.

Cabin – Private accommodation on board a ship; also called a *stateroom*. Large cabins are often referred to as *suites*. An *outside cabin* is one with a porthole, window or veranda. An *inside cabin* has no porthole or window.

Crew-to-passenger ratio – This helps determine the level of service on board a ship. For example, a ship carrying 500 crew and 1000 passengers has a ratio of 1 crew member for every 2 passengers. Note: The passenger capacity quoted for each ship in Chapter 5's directory is based on double occupancy of all cabins.

Cruise-only fare – The price showing that of the cruise and excluding all extras such as taxes, port charges, air fares, tips and so on.

Double occupancy – The rate per person for cabins capable of accommodating two people. For a single person to occupy such a cabin the charge ranges from 120 to 200 per cent of the per person fare and is referred to as a single supplement.

Embarkation – Entering or boarding the ship; leaving the ship is **disembarkation**.

Flag of Convenience – A ship is often registered outside its country of administration and this is done for financial reasons.

Flagship – The best, oldest, newest or biggest ship in a cruise line's fleet.

Forward – Near or at the **bow** (front) of the ship.

Itinerary – The exact dates and route of a cruise, including port of embarkation and disembarkation, and all ports of call visited in between. Cruise lines are constantly fine-tuning and altering their itineraries so a particular ship may not be on a cruise you want or stop at all the ports it did from a previous year. To check a line's upcoming itineraries, talk to your travel agent.

Knots – The speed of a ship calculated by distance traveled, in nautical miles, in the space of an hour. A nautical mile is equal to 1.15 land miles.

Lido Deck – An upper stern deck containing a pool and restaurant.

Line Voyages – Cruises that begin at one port and end at another.

Loop Cruises – The ship departs from and returns to the same port, which is referred to as the *home port* or *base port*.

Port Side – The left side of the ship when facing the **bow** (forward).

Port taxes – Charges levied by the authorities at some ports of call, usually payable by the individual passenger and sometimes included in the final price of the cruise.

Repositioning Cruises – When cruise ships travel from one major cruising area to another with stops along the way at various ports. (For example, a ship travelling from the Caribbean at the end of the winter season to Alaska or Europe for the summer season.)

Ratings – A ship's rating is determined by its level of accommodations, facilities, meals, maintenance and service.

Sister Ships – Ships that are identical in basic design and construction but usually with variations in internal layout, decor and public room features.

Space Ratio – A measure of how roomy or crowded a ship is. The ship's tonnage (total space capacity) divided by the total number of passengers equals the space ratio. 40+ is the ultimate in spaciousness; -20 is high density.

Stabilizer – A wing-like appendage which sticks out from either side of the ship and is adjusted to help keep the ship level.

Starboard Side – The right side of the ship when facing the **bow** (forward).

Steward – A waiter or cabin attendant.

Tonnage – The overall size and capacity of the ship. A ship that measures more than 30,000 tons is a 'large' ship; 20,000 to 30,000 tons is a 'medium' ship; and one less than 20,000 tons is 'small'. Ships that measure 70,000+ tons are called 'megaships'.

Index